PRAISE FOR *THE GREAT GOOD THING*
AND FOR ANDREW KLAVAN

"Andrew Klavan's superb new book deserves to become a classic of its kind. Klavan's immense talents as a writer are on full view in what must certainly rank as his most important book to date. *Tolle lege.*"
—Eric Metaxas, #1 *New York Times* bestselling author of *Bonhoeffer* and *If You Can Keep It*

"The most original American novelist of crime and suspense since Cornell Woolrich."
—Stephen King

"A master storyteller"
—Clive Cussler

"Klavan does tough-guy heroes and sexual tension better than anyone writing today."
—Janet Evanovich

"Klavan, who has a perfect sense of timing, delivers all the cliff-hangers and hairpin turns that you want from a beat-the-clock suspense thriller."
—*The New York Times Book Review*

"Klavan's writing is masterful and his characters superbly drawn."
—*Forbes*

"A major talent . . . Klavan's understanding of the human heart and how it can be torn or salved by eros is uncanny."
—*Publishers Weekly*

THE
GREAT
GOOD
THING

Other Books by Andrew Klavan

THE
GREAT
GOOD
THING

*A Secular Jew
Comes to Faith in Christ*

ANDREW KLAVAN

NELSON
BOOKS

An Imprint of Thomas Nelson

Published in Nashville, Tennessee, by Nelson Books, an imprint of Thomas Nelson. Nelson Books and Thomas Nelson are registered trademarks of HarperCollins Christian Publishing, Inc.

Published in association with Trident Media Group, LLC, 41 Madison Avenue, 36th floor, New York, New York 10010.

Thomas Nelson titles may be purchased in bulk for educational, business, fund-raising, or sales promotional use. For information, please e-mail SpecialMarkets@ThomasNelson.com.

Library of Congress Cataloging-in-Publication Data

Names: Klavan, Andrew, author.

Title: The great good thing : a secular Jew comes to faith in Christ / Andrew Klavan.

Description: Nashville : Thomas Nelson, 2016.

Identifiers: LCCN 2015048997 | ISBN 9780718017347

Subjects: LCSH: Klavan, Andrew. | Jews--Conversion to Christianity.

Classification: LCC BV2623.K538 A3 2016 | DDC 248.2/466092--dc23 LC record available at http://lccn.loc.gov/2015048997

Printed in the United States of America

16 17 18 19 20 RRD 6 5 4 3 2

This book is for Peter Henry Moore:
"Remarkable boy . . . delightful boy!"

"FIRE. God of Abraham, God of Isaac, God of Jacob, not of philosophers and scholars. Certitude, heartfelt joy, peace. God of Jesus Christ . . . My God and your God. . . . Joy, Joy, Joy, tears of joy . . ."

—MATHEMATICIAN AND PHILOSOPHER BLAISE PASCAL, FROM HIS NOTE TO HIMSELF AFTER HIS CONVERSION. HE KEPT IT SEWN IN HIS COAT, WHERE IT WAS FOUND AFTER HIS DEATH.

CONTENTS

INTRODUCTION

The Church of the Incarnation stands on the corner of 35th Street and Madison Avenue in Manhattan. Like any fine old church in so massive and so contemporary a metropolis, it seems out of place, out of time. The nineteenth-century brownstone spire is dwarfed by the featureless wall of the modern building slapped up beside it, a narrow flat-faced slab of an apartment tower that looks like it might keel over sideways at any moment and squash the house of worship flat. Likewise, the noise of the traffic on the frantic avenue at its doorstep makes a joke of the church's promise of tranquility. With the homicidal screech-and-careen of yellow taxis and the workaday flatulence of uptown buses and the angry honk of horns and even the machine-gun footsteps of the pedestrians as they go racing past—with all that tumult, all that noise—the present business of the city seems to drown out any whisper of eternity.

But then, you step through the church's doors and all that is gone. It's quiet inside, the cool, hollow, uncanny quiet of old churches everywhere. Beyond the brighter narthex—the lobby to you and me—the nave is vast and dark. The solemn shadows are touched here and there with blue and golden ghost-light, will-o'-the-wisps created by the indirect sun on the stained-glass windows. The windows—by such master-shops as Tiffany, William Morris, and Clayton and Bell—are the pride of the place. Jesus summoning Lazarus from the tomb. Moses bringing the law from the mountain. Paul preaching to the Athenians on Mars Hill. A dozen windows like that— more—arrayed along the walls, above the stolid oaken pews, between the reedy Corinthian columns, down to the marble altar and rising, finally, over the altar's Caen stone screen. The four evangelists, fitted with wings, are sculpted on the screen amid elaborate tracery. Three cherubs carry a banner that reads: *And the Word was made flesh and dwelt among us.*

The baptismal font is below the altar, down on pew level, off to the left. It's almost hidden away there in the dim spaces beneath the carved oaken pulpit. Which is a shame. It's a beautiful thing. There's a mosaic bowl and, above that, a graceful bronze statue of the boy John the Baptist, a youth clothed in camel hair, his left hand holding a reed, his right hand raised in benediction.

Ten years ago—almost exactly ten years as I'm writing—I came to this building on an early evening in May—came through the traffic to this church, came through the narthex to this nave, came down the aisle beneath the ghost-lit windows and approached the bronze Baptist in the altar shadows. There were four people waiting for me. Doug Ousley, one of my oldest friends and the church rector, was dressed for business in his gray priest get-up with the turnaround collar. Mary, Doug's wife, whom I dearly loved, was slumped in her wheelchair, wrapped in a scarf against the cold of the surrounding stones: an irrepressibly vivacious woman once, worn down now by decades of wasting disease. Their sons, John and Andrew, were a couple of strapping blond and heroically handsome lads, both like nephews to me. Doug had agreed to open his church after hours to indulge my desire for privacy, so these were all the witnesses I had.

It was the day after my father's memorial. He had died about a month before. My wife and son and daughter had already flown back home to California, but I had stayed on alone for a few days. For this.

I was forty-nine years old and about to be baptized a Christian.

No one could have been more surprised than I was. I never thought I was the type. I had been born and raised a Jew and lived most of my life as an agnostic. I believed in the fullest freedom of thought into the widest reaches of fact and philosophy. I believed in science and analysis and reasonable explanations. I had no time for magical thinking of any kind. I couldn't bear solemn piety. I despised even the ordinary varieties of willful blindness to the tragic shambles of life on earth. And as for what the philosopher Schopenhauer once called the Christian's "banal optimism"—that forced, praise-singing cheer in the face of pain and disappointment and inescapable death—oh God, how I hated it; it set my teeth on edge.

I was—I am—a worldling by nature. I was delighted by the world, by which I don't mean just the sunshine, trees, and twittering bluebirds but also sex, money, gossip, a good single malt, the crooked hilarity of politics, and the bizarre little lies and betrayals that make up our relationships, especially our relationships with ourselves. This was the stuff of the novels I wrote and the novels I read, of the plays and movies I went to and the television I watched, not to mention the news stories and histories that made me shake my head and laugh at the everlasting circus of human corruption. This was the stuff of drama and vitality to me, character writ in action good and bad. I'd met Christians from time to time who said they couldn't wait to die and go to heaven. Not me. I liked it here. I found it amusing. If I had any idea of paradise at all, it was as some celestial home theater in which I got to kick back forever with a Scotch and some cashew nuts and channel-surf the mad spectacle of existence to see how it all turned out in the end.

And if my realism and worldliness didn't keep me from baptism, there was the even greater obstacle of who I was—my cultural identity, let's call it. I belonged to what the British refer to as the chattering classes. I thought and wrote and created stories for a living. I was one of the men of the coasts and cities, at home among the snarks and cynics of these postmodern times. By rights, my attitude toward religion should have been the same as theirs: at its harshest, a disdain for the irrational survival of a primitive superstition; or in milder and more tolerant moods, a wistful regret over the demise of a comforting delusion and pass the Chardonnay. I do enjoy a good Chardonnay.

To kneel instead before this marble font, beneath the upraised hand of this bronze boy John, to declare in this church that Jesus Christ was Lord and to accept the uniquely salvific truth of his life and preaching, death and resurrection—this, it seemed to me even in the moment, was to renounce my natural place in the age, to turn against my upbringing and my kind. It felt, so help me, as if I were flinging myself off the deck of a holiday cruise ship, falling away from its lighted ballrooms and casinos, from the parties and the music and the sparkling wine of Fashionable Ideas, to go plunging down and down and did I mention down into a wave-tossed theological solitude.

When it first came to me that I should be baptized—that I had to be, really, in the name of integrity, if nothing else—I entered a five-month-long agony of self-examination. How could I be certain in my faith? What did I believe, in fact, and why? In a world of science and technology, where a physical cause could be found for every spiritual phenomenon, where even our thoughts and emotions could be reduced to electrochemical reactions in the brain, what had led me to embrace a two-thousand-year-old religion of sin and souls and miracles and heavenly redemption? Had I stumbled on the hallelujah truth, or just gone mad—or, that is, had I gone mad again? I'd been through that maze of mirrors once before. That was a central part of my story.

These were hard questions to answer, maybe impossible.

Because if there's one thing every good novelist understands, it's that our inner world is unreliable and yet there's no getting beyond it. Every sense is subject to deception, including the moral sense. What seems at first like the hard surface of spiritual reality is really fathomless when you dive down into it. There is no bottom. We never know anything for sure.

This was one of the central subjects of the thrillers I wrote, one of their recurring themes. My heroes were always desperately on the run, desperately trying to get at a truth that baffled their assumptions and philosophies. In *Don't Say a Word*, a psychiatrist expertly analyzes the paranoid delusions of a beautiful schizophrenic only to discover that her delusions are more trustworthy than his analysis. In *Animal Hour*, a woman finds that her everyday life is a hallucination while her hallucinations are her only clues to reality. In *True Crime*, a Christian prisoner awaiting execution faces the meaningless emptiness of death while an atheist reporter blurts out an instinctive prayer that leads the way to a miracle. In all my books, my characters raced against time to explain the world while the world eluded them. Some deadly reality was always closing in around them as they chased after the illusion up ahead.

In telling these stories, it turned out, of course, that I wasn't just exploring the problem as a writer; I was also wrestling with it as a man. What was truth? How could you know it? How could you think, live, and make choices and judgments day by day if you didn't know?

Slowly, over the years, as I wrote and as I read, and as I did think and live and make choices and judgments day by day, it began to seem to me that this philosophical dilemma—the dilemma that caused and defined many of the political and cultural battles of the postmodern era—had been implanted in the conscience of the West by one book of our essential literature: *The Gospel According to St. John*. The oldest fragment of New Testament papyrus we have preserves the question of the sophisticated Roman official Pontius Pilate as he sits in judgment over the backwoods Jewish preacher Jesus of Nazareth: "What is truth?" The Gospel's weird answer has already been spoken by Jesus elsewhere in the narrative. "I am the way and the truth and the life," he says.

I am the truth. What does that even mean? Here was another thing that always annoyed me about religion. Believers would make these proclamations—*Jesus is the Truth! Jesus is the Way!*—and their eyes would glow bright and their throats would get all swollen with ecstasy, and I would be thinking, *Huh? What? Jesus is the truth? How? In what sense? What on earth are you talking about?* I could never make heads or tails of it.

And yet, here I was, nearing fifty, and I had been seized by the startling conviction that I should be baptized. There had been no flash of light on the road to Damascus, no *tolle lege* under the fig tree. Jesus had not appeared to me as I lay drunk in the gutter—not that I remembered anyway. There had only been a slow dawning of awareness that had solidified into the certainty that I was a Christian. But why? Did I now believe that Jesus was, in fact, the answer to the question, what is Truth? What did I mean by that? And how had I reached that conclusion?

About five years before, after a lifetime of agnosticism, I had come to believe in God. It started as a tentative experiment in prayer. Soon I was praying every day and the experience was undeniably powerful and transformative. I could see that praying had improved my life in any number of ways and so I was committed to it. But there was no system of thought attached to the practice, no church, no documents of any authority—nothing even particularly supernatural, if you except the presence of God himself. I had to admit there had been some amazingly immediate and practical responses to my prayers at times, but those could have easily been dismissed as coincidences rather than miracles. Really, the whole prayer endeavor might have been explained away as a sort of self-improvement system of meditation-out-loud. For me personally, yes, it sure seemed as if there were a God on the other end of the prayer-line. I had come to believe there was. But, when you came right down to it, what difference did it make? Prayer worked, so I prayed. I wasn't going to argue the mechanics of it with anyone.

To take my beliefs to the level of baptism, though—that was different. That implied an entire range of concepts and conclusions I wasn't sure about at all. Just how specific, how biblical, was I planning to get here? Had I come to accept the fall of man? Was I ready to proclaim the Incarnation? Did I seriously believe that a carpenter had risen from the dead on Easter? I'd never even seen one go to work on Sunday!

I was living with my wife and children in a town called Montecito then. It's a famously beautiful place, a well-to-do Southern California suburb of the city of Santa Barbara, about eighty miles north of LA. My office was in Santa Barbara proper, in the middle of town. I drove there every morning, avoiding the freeway, keeping to the back roads. It took about ten to fifteen minutes, depending on my route. I did a lot of my praying as I drove along.

Now, as the idea of baptism took hold within me, as I began to question myself, as I began to question God about what was happening to me, I started to take longer and longer detours to give myself more time for prayer and reflection. I steered my car up into the hills, along narrow, winding switchbacks through coyote country, hillside rising to my right while to my left the brown earth sloped away into a green and brilliant panorama of one of the most spectacular cityscapes in the country—in the world. Forest flecked with colonnaded mansions, boulevards lined with stately buildings of bright-white stone, red Spanish tiles on rooftops everywhere, the curling coastline and the glittering bay and the sea and the sea mist and the islands in the misty distance . . .

But I drove without looking. Or that is, I was looking inward only, asking myself again and again: What did I believe and why and how had I come to it and was I sure, could I ever be sure? Was I just deifying my own neuroses somehow? Was I turning to Christ as some sort of late-in-life rebellion against my father? Or was I looking to heaven for the fatherly acceptance I never had on earth? Was I running away from my Jewish identity, trying to escape bigotry and cultural clichés through religious assimilation? Or was this some sort of horrifying relapse, after two happy decades, into the craziness of my youth when, for a brief period, I had embraced a loony-tune piety before cracking up completely?

I had become like a character in one of my own stories, desperately trying to unknit the fabric of fact and perception, to separate the warp of psychology from the weft of objective truth, before time ran out. My commute to work became twenty minutes long, then thirty, forty-five minutes, then an hour, sometimes more, as I harrowed my soul with interrogations.

There was a lot at stake. So it seemed to me at any rate. I don't mean salvation—heaven over hell. I wasn't thinking in those terms at all. But my life. What effect would baptism have on my life?

There would be no hiding it, that was for sure. I was a writer. I had no secrets. I hadn't had a thought in years that hadn't ended up in print somewhere. If I became a Christian I would be bound to declare it in some article or some interview or something. And what then? Would I lose work because of it? At the time, I was making good money in Hollywood, turning out ghost-story scripts and murder mysteries. Would producers stop considering me for such assignments? Would they assume I was too pious to produce rollicking good tales about masked madmen with butcher knives chasing half-naked women across the screen?

And would I *become* too pious, in fact? What a nightmare

that would be! As a writer, I prided myself on seeing and describing the world as it was, not as I wanted it or thought it was supposed to be. I had made my living writing hard-boiled fiction about tough, cynical men and femmes fatales swept up in ugly underworlds of crime, sex, and murder. Would I suddenly be reduced to penning saccharine fluff about some little girl who lost her pet bunny but Jesus brought it back again? "Oh, God," I prayed fervently more than once, "whatever happens, don't let me become a Christian novelist!"

Even that prospect, terrible as it was, was only a part of the greater danger. If I became a Christian, would I lose my freedom of thought? Would I sacrifice my ability to question every proposition and examine every belief to the bone? Would I lose my realism and my tragic sensibility? Would I descend into that smiley-faced religious idiocy that mistakes the good health and prosperity of the moment for the supernatural favor of God?

These were not just academic questions. I was living a good life now, and I was content, but that hadn't always been the case. I'd been miserable and twisted as a young man, angry and soul-sick and mired in foolish delusions. My sanity had been hard fought for and hard won. Reality mattered to me: it was the medicine that kept me well. I had no desire whatsoever to cling to any comforting lies, or to any lies at all. I had no desire whatsoever to believe in a God who wasn't there.

Then, too, there was the matter of my Jewish identity, surely as big a stumbling block as any. I had never been a religious Jew. I had been forced to go to Hebrew School as a child, and I had been bar-mitzvahed at thirteen. But I had hated the Jewish rite of passage, not for itself but because it was an act of hypocrisy in my case. I had rejected the faith—and all faith—not long afterward.

Still, a Jew I remained, racially and culturally. I had the face for it, no question, and the wise-guy urban attitudes, the love of intellection and debate, and the irreverent sense of humor, an almost pathological inability to take myself or anyone else seriously. I knew the history of my people well and identified with it: both our miraculous triumphs and achievements and the correspondingly demonic hatred we inspired. I was proud when a Jew won a Nobel Prize or hit a home run. And I never let an ugly remark go unanswered, or tried to pass myself off as anything other than what I was.

If I had any discomfort with my Jewishness, it arose in the face of cultural clichés, the sort of stereotypes that were circulated as often by other Jews as by gentiles. I didn't like to see Jews in books and movies routinely portrayed as weak or cowardly, incompetent with machinery or uncomfortable with the outdoors. I wasn't anything like that. I'd been in plenty of schoolyard duke-outs as a kid and proved I could take a punch and throw one. Like my father before me, I could fix pretty much anything given the right tools. And I'd been an outdoorsman, camping and fishing and hiking, much of my life. I didn't like it when Jews were described as cosmopolitan either, unattached citizens of the world. Me, I was American through and through. I was born here, and a patriot to my bones.

But to turn away from my Jewish heritage—even to seem to turn away—to join what many of my fellow Jews considered the religion of the enemy—was no small thing, not to me. I had thought and read and written a good deal about the causes and effects of anti-Semitism, and for a time I had wholly immersed myself in studying the unfathomable wickedness of the Holocaust. No thinking person would call such cruelties "Christian," but likewise no one could deny the historic role and responsibility of the church in this inextinguishable hatred and its resulting atrocities. It was the default belief of many Jews that a Jew who converted was trying to exempt himself from that hostility, trying to ingratiate himself with his gentile oppressors. ("They'll still throw you in the ovens," was the immediate response of one Jewish friend when I told him about my baptism.) I was a public man. I wrote and said things and people read and heard them. I did not want anyone, anywhere, ever to think I had betrayed my people, the greatest and most persecuted among the nations of the earth.

And I knew there was one person who would believe exactly that, one person who would think me a coward and a traitor to my kind, without question, without a doubt: my father. We were not friends, my father and I, and there were many times through the years when we had been at daggers drawn. We lived on opposite coasts. We didn't see each other much. We rarely spoke and, when we did, I never told him more than the most superficial news about my life. But he was old now, and I was middle-aged. We were both good men, or tried to be. We were both men of integrity, or tried to be. He had been a kind and generous grandfather to my children, and there had been peace and even amicability between us for at least a decade. My baptism would end that peace, I was certain. My father had once told me he would disown me if I ever converted. I knew he would never forgive me. I hated the thought of bringing trouble to my house.

For five months, winter into spring, I drove the hills of Santa Barbara and prayed. I questioned my sincerity and my intentions. I analyzed the philosophical steps that had led me to the brink of conversion, holding them to the light one after another like a jeweler with a set of gems, turning each one this way and that to study its facets and pronounce upon its qualities. I reviewed the experiences that had gone into my decision. I tried to tell myself the story of my life as a novelist would tell it, highlighting the formative moments, exposing the ways in which personal history shaped my ideas and possibly distorted my view of the world. And because I am a novelist, and because books I've read and books I've written have molded my mind as much as the events I've lived through and the people I've met, I revisited and reconsidered the stories and poems and works of philosophy that had meant the most to me, the authors who had served as my invisible mentors through a life in which living mentors had been in short supply.

This memoir is, to some extent, that long meditation remembered. I don't mean it to be an autobiography or a psychological confession or anything like that. It records my memory of things, even when it might be faulty, because my memory guided me at the time. It's definitely not intended as an exposé of my own sins or anyone else's; I hope to leave out as many of both as possible! I've also tried to tiptoe quietly around the private lives of anyone who did not directly affect my ultimate decision, especially the lives of my brothers, three men I love and admire, who have the right to remember our shared family history in their own ways. Nor am I trying to preach or argue with or prove anything to anyone. I'm not a theologian or a philosopher. I'm just a barefoot teller of tales, as I frequently explain to my long-suffering wife. Anyway, God is not susceptible to proofs and disproofs. If you believe, the evidence is all around you. If you don't believe, no evidence can be enough.

All the same, I feel the need to explain myself to myself, to set my reasons down on the page where I can look them over. Other men are born into their faith and never leave it. I was planted elsewhere and had to find my way. And when my five-month pilgrimage through the Santa Barbara hills was done, I came home rejoicing. I was convinced and fully convinced: my mind was God's, my soul was Christ's, my faith was true. How had that happened and why? Given the spiritual distance I'd traveled, given the depths of my doubts, given the darkness of my most uncertain places, and given, most of all, the elation and wonder I felt at the journey's end, it seems to me a story worth telling.

CHAPTER 1

GREAT NECK JEW

The town I grew up in is named Great Neck. It is situated on a peninsula on the north shore of Long Island, about twenty-five miles east of Manhattan. It was, in my boyhood, as it is today, a wealthy town, a well-tailored suburban refuge from the swarming city.

The riches here weren't inherited, they were earned. Great Neck had been associated with new money at least since the twenties, when F. Scott Fitzgerald used parts of it as the inspiration for the West Egg of his novel *The Great Gatsby*. In my teens, I dated a girl who lived in a mansion that sat pretty near where Gatsby's sat, if not on the very spot. I remember chasing her once through the high grass on the flatlands below her hilltop home, breaking out into the open to catch her on the shore of Manhasset Bay. "*There*," she said breathlessly, as I wrapped my arms around her. Pointing across the dark water, she told me: There was Sands Point, the East Egg of the novel, where the green light had shone. Gatsby, a self-made man, a bootlegger with aspirations toward elegance, would often gaze across the water at that spot, as we were doing now. He would dream of finding his lost love Daisy and of entering her world of old money and sophistication and class.

Great Neck had changed since those days, but in many ways, Gatsby's dream was still alive there. After World War II, the sons and daughters of Jewish immigrants who, like their gentile predecessors, had made enough money to leave the city, began to move out to the luxurious suburb. By the late fifties, when my father—a rising New York disc jockey with a popular morning show—brought his young family there, the town was a haven for newly rich Jews. And like the newly rich Gatsby, they were in love with the dream of WASP American elegance and wanted to become an accepted part of the mainstream and the upper rung.

The result was the town I grew up in—to all appearances a high-end version of the classic 1950s suburb, a place that could have sprung to life from one of the popular television situation comedies of those days: *Father Knows Best, The Donna Reed Show, Leave It to Beaver, Ozzie and Harriet. The Dick Van Dyke Show,* in fact, was written and produced by two old friends of my father's and involved a character like the comedian Sid Caesar, himself a Great Neck resident. The show's central family, while not based on my family, bore similarities to us, with its mixture of showbiz temperament and suburban normalcy.

These happy-go-lucky sitcoms edited every trace of

dysfunction out of the world I knew. That was a distortion obviously—an ideal. But the ideal and the reality played off each other. The TV shows looked like Great Neck and, consciously or not, Great Neck modeled itself on the shows. Maybe in our real families, Father didn't always know Best. Maybe he wouldn't have known Best if Best rose up and bit him on the leg! But he caught the train to the city every morning. He paid the bills and kept the lights burning, mowed the lawn and fixed the car and backed up mother's discipline with his fearsome presence: he was a father. Maybe real-life Mom didn't vacuum the house flawlessly arrayed in pearls and a pleated skirt like the mother on *Leave It to Beaver*. Maybe she flirted with the milkman or waited for the kids to go to bed so she could hammer back a couple of mugs of vodka pretending it was tea. But she was there to greet us when we came home from school in the afternoon. She made us dinner, kept watch on us through the kitchen window, put Band-Aids on our scrapes and bruises. She was Mom and that was no small thing, not to us. Likewise big brothers who hit you with a pillow on television, hit you in real life so hard with their fists you saw stars and bluebirds. And little sisters who were virgin princesses on the small screen were harpies from hell on a bad day in the big world. All the same, they were brothers; they were sisters. They did what siblings do: drive you crazy, hurt you, love you, show you the way. The ideal suburbs of TV sitcoms were a fiction, but there was enough truth in that fiction to allow us to recognize our lives.

So Great Neck was a suburb, like all the other suburbs

around the country that inspired the television shows that, in turn, inspired us. But in Great Neck, the Great Neck of my childhood, there was one central difference. In those other towns, and in those TV towns that represented them, when Sundays came, the moms and daughters in their best dresses and the dads and sons wearing suits and ties and slicked-back hair would head for church. In Great Neck, the Sabbath was Saturday, and we went to synagogue. We knew this made us different from our Christian counterparts, but we also saw, again, that it looked very much the same.

It was *supposed* to look the same. It was supposed to *be* the same, for all intents and purposes. All the cultural machinery of the town was geared toward blending that local discrepancy into the greater national culture. With families named Bernstein and Levine and Schwartz living on streets named Chadwick, Andover, Old Colony, and Piccadilly, Great Neck was a sort of gigantic contraption engineered to assimilate upper-middle-class Jews into the predominant Protestant-American society around them. If there was any potential conflict between our two cultural identities—if we even *had* two cultural identities—no one told us so, no one outside our homes anyway, no one I knew.

Sure, there were families that were more religious than mine, more rooted in their Jewishness. There were houses where some grandparent with an accent and a grudge kept the Old World hostilities alive and kicking. But not outside, not on the rolling lawns, not on the happy anglophile Great Neck streets, not for me or for my friends. For us, in school, when we were taught about "our history," it was American history. When we learned about "our forefathers," they were the American founders. Until I was eleven or so, I thought I was a direct descendant of George Washington and Ben Franklin and Thomas Jefferson. To my mind, they were as much my ancestors as Moses and David and the rest of the biblical gang.

Then, as now, I never thought of myself as anything but American. My values were American values: freedom above all things, live-and-let-live tolerance, truth, justice, fair play. My games were American games. My heroes were the same as the heroes of the other kids around the country: astronauts and Davy Crockett, baseball players, Superman and the president. What's more, since so many of the kids I knew were Jewish, most of the typical characters in an American kid's life were, in my life, also Jews. In a gentile town, maybe the odd Jewish kid or two would stand out. Maybe they'd have been relegated to stereotypical Jewish roles: outsiders, scholars, yeshiva boys, swots. But in my town, the high school football heroes were Jews and the lover boys were Jews and so were the beauty queens and the hoydens and many of the delinquents as well. When we were little at least, the idea that our Jewishness might somehow prevent us from being fully American—from being fully what we so obviously were—simply did not exist among the kids I knew.

Nor did it ever occur to us—it never occurred to me, anyway—that any differences between the Jewish and gentile kids in town were due to race or religion. Great Neck's population was about 50 percent Jewish. And while the Jews tended to cluster together in their neighborhoods, the gentile kids at school were never excluded, or even noted as gentile. That my one or two gentile pals went to church on Sunday or had pictures of Jesus in their houses were matters of interest, but not very much interest really.

There was no racial animosity among us that I saw. There was hardly even any racial awareness. I was thirty years old—literally thirty—before I realized that a certain number of the fistfights I had gotten into in junior high school had begun when some large Polish Catholic lummox had started picking on some smaller Jewish geek. At the time, there had been no appearance of anything racial or religious in the conflict. No one had slung any racial slurs or taunts in either direction. It was just a big guy picking on a little guy, that's all I knew.

I was aware there was such a thing as anti-Semitism. Of course I was: my father was obsessed with it, increasingly obsessed as the years went on. The Holocaust had ended not twenty years before. So, sure, we all knew it was there. But it was a foreign thing, we thought, and a thing of the past. I never actually experienced it as a little kid. Not once. When I was fifteen or sixteen, during one of the very last fights I was ever in, my opponent called me a *kike*. That was the first time that had ever happened. Even then, it seemed only tangentially connected to my Jewish identity. The fight hadn't been about that. The guy's girlfriend had been flirting with me over a pinball game in the local bowling alley. The guy had gotten tough about it and we stepped outside to settle the matter. As the guy's punk friends encircled us, shouting, we duked it out and I got the better of him. He screamed the slur after me as I walked away. I was startled—I'd never heard the word used seriously before—but I shrugged it off. Nowadays people get hysterical over such "hate speech." But really, let's face it, you have to have *some* nasty thing to call your enemies. If I'd been Irish or black or Italian, the kid would have called me something else. I didn't think he hated Jews. I still don't think so. I just think he hated getting dusted in front of his pals.

No. I was an American. In Great Neck, we were all Americans. We said the Pledge of Allegiance to the flag every morning in school. We went to the Fourth of July parade. We played baseball and watched baseball on TV and collected baseball cards and traded them and gambled them in a million different makeshift games. When I was seven and the New York Yankees' Roger Maris broke Babe Ruth's home run record, I jumped up and down on my bed, cheering, as the news came over the radio (even though I was secretly a little disappointed it hadn't been my hero Mickey Mantle who'd won the day). When I was nine and a boy rushed into our fourth-grade classroom to announce that "the Reds killed Kennedy," that was my president who had been murdered, my nation that mourned, my world, the only world I knew, that had turned upside-down. I was an American, through and through. I am one still.

That was why so many decades later, when I felt myself called to faith in Jesus Christ, when, distraught and in confusion, I drove up into the mountains to question the integrity of my convictions, to cross-examine my motives day after day, week after week, month after month, I had to ask myself: Was this a real religious conversion or was it merely the final stage in the process of assimilation that had begun in my home-town so long ago? Was I putting on the whole armor of God or merely joining the church of the majority?

Are you a Jew?

From time to time, someone in the wider world would ask this question of a Great Neck teenager. And so often, he or she would answer, "Well, my parents are."

Well, my parents are. Or as Jonathan Miller put it in the British comedy revue *Beyond the Fringe,* "I'm not really a Jew. Just Jew-ish. I never went the whole hog." Jew-ish, that's it. A lot of us Great Neckers said some version of that in our teens. As we came into that age when people begin to think seriously about who they are, being a Jew just felt like, you know, our parents' thing, yesterday's thing, history's, not today's. We had not become ashamed of our Jewishness exactly. It had simply begun to seem alien to us, archaic, extraneous. The turn-of-the-century Russian *shtetl* Jews in the exuberant musical *Fiddler on the Roof*—which hit Broadway when I was ten years old—could sing about the joys of "Tradition!" all they liked. But what traditions were they talking about exactly? A smothering, claustrophobic ghetto, estranged from the soci-ety around it? An ancient language no one else spoke written in antiquated letters no one else could read? Funny-looking skullcaps? Corkscrew sidelocks? Over-long beards?

Tradition might have been some consolation for our grandfathers in the Old Country. In the Old Country, they had been strangers in a strange land, hated and excluded by the natives. But what did we need it here for, in glorious America? Here, everyone was a stranger and so everyone was part of the mix. Thanks for the Hebrew lesson and the yarmulke, Rabbi, real nice, but oh look, my fellow American just planted my flag on the moon! My flag! On the moon! See you later, Rabbi.

Are you a Jew?

Well, my parents are. Jew-ish.

For each of us, in every *Leave It to Beaver* house, on Oxford Boulevard and on Plymouth and Cambridge and Hampshire Roads, the path to all-American selfhood was bound to pass through such areas of shadow. They were like the half-lit corridors and corners in a psychic maze from which, with any luck, we would emerge into the light of an integrated cultural identity.

For me, in my house, in my family, it was a maze of multiple dimensions, some passageways haunted, some corners dark.

My parents despised Great Neck in many ways. They constantly spoke of moving—to Manhattan, to California, overseas—but somehow never did, never could. My mother, I suspect, would have hit the road in a heartbeat, given free rein. She didn't particularly take to playing Just Mommy in the suburbs. She loved bright lights and Broadway shows and wanted to live in the city. But my dad was not the traveling kind. Once planted, he stayed. And as he became one of the most popular DJs in the city, living in the high-end suburb felt like success to him, even when it got on his nerves. Still, both he and Mom exhibited a degree of disdain for the town they raised us in, and they taught us, their four sons, to disdain it too. They wanted us to be in it, but not of it.

Our neighbors were *nouveau riche*, they told us. They were tradesmen who had earned their money later in life. They didn't know how to handle their wealth with the panache of the aristocracy. The irony of hearing this from my dad and mom—the son of a pawnbroker and the daughter of a disbarred ambulance-chasing lawyer who had to move house every other month to beat the landlord—somehow never occurred to us boys, or at least not to me. All I knew was the fact—and it was a fact—that my parents were indeed more urbane, more elegant, more sophisticated, more *classy* than the parents of many of my friends.

My friends' parents drove insanely massive Cadillacs, each one two tons of garish flash that seemed to take up both lanes on Great Neck's narrow horse-and-buggy roads. My dad, conversely, brought home a chic succession of European compacts: a Citroen, an MG, several Volvos, and the like. Many of my friends lived in mansions with columned porticoes and swimming pools on their acres of land. We had a relatively modest colonial clapboard, gracefully decorated inside by my mother who really did have excellent taste. When we were teenagers, Dad had an asphalt badminton court built in our backyard. But no pool. Never a pool. Pools were garish. *Nouveau riche.*

Pools were garish and too much jewelry was garish. Fur coats and overly colorful shirts and talking too loud and talking about how much money you had—all *nouveau riche*. Rambunctious boys though we were, my brothers and I had good manners when we needed them. We learned to speak softly—oh, and most importantly, we never ever spoke with a New York or Long Island accent.

A NuYawk accent! Or, heaven help us, a Lawn Guyland accent—that squawking horror of a dialect that gave the Guyland its nickname! As an up-and-coming performer on both TV and radio, my father had trained any hint of localism out of his voice. An expert at imitating accents and dialects of all kinds, he claimed he could no longer speak in the manner of his native Baltimore (*Balmer!*) because he had labored so long to unlearn it. He and my mother passed this speech training onto their sons with a passion. No closed vowel or dropped *g* that escaped our lips went uncorrected. We were told to repeat the phrase, "My family is in a class by itself," not just so as to incorporate the truth of its meaning (as I later realized), but to drill us out of anything that sounded even remotely like, "Muy fehmly is in a clehss buy itself." To this day, my children tease me because I say *chahklet* and *dahnkey* rather than *chocolate* and *donkey*, having worked so hard as a lad not to say *chawklet* or *dawnkey*. Often as I've tried, I find I can't make the adjustment.

All this attention to gentility had its benefits, of course. There's certainly nothing wrong with having good manners. Good diction comes in handy too. And no one ever died from having understated tastes in decor and clothing.

But my parents' commitment to our elegance as a family

was always stated in opposition to the perceived inelegance of the families around us—the families of our friends, the only people we knew. Ultimately, I think, this contributed to an insular and contrarian misanthropy in us boys. We developed the absurd sense that we were somehow superior to "ordinary people." And given our circumstances, that meant we were superior to ordinary Jews.

This snobbery—and its underlying racism—emanated mostly from my mother. Despite his hostility toward the world in general, my father was a democratic fellow at heart. He knew where he came from and had no pretensions to aristocracy. For him, I think, teaching us genteel behavior and uninflected diction was a matter of show biz more than anything else. As a performer, he wanted us to be presentable to the largest possible audience.

In my mother, however—my tasteful, elegant, and sophisticated mother—for whom taste, elegance, and sophistication were qualities of the utmost value—the whole training program smacked of anti-Semitism. She did have . . . not pretensions exactly. *Aspirations* would be closer to the truth. She had spent long hours of her unhappy youth playing hooky, ensconced in movie theaters, watching sparkling, chic stars swan across the flickering screen. Katharine Hepburn, Bette Davis, Ginger Rogers. That was who she wanted to be like, I think. Upper-crust Englishmen and WASP college professors—they were as gods to her. And, of course, Franklin Delano Roosevelt. With his four terms, he was president for her entire girlhood. Even when she was well into her eighties, you only had to mention his name—you only had to mention his initials—to evoke her Pavlovian gasp of admiration: "Ah, he spoke the King's English!" She loved that sort of thing.

She would have sent us to fancy private schools, if my father would've plunked for it. She would have had us wearing tennis-anyone whites and country-club blue blazers with crests on the pockets, though what the crests would have been I can't for the life of me imagine. To her, Great Neck was not just a town full of *nouveau riche*. It was a town, specifically, full of *nouveau riche* Jews. The fancy cars, the jewelry, the brash voices with their Guyland bray: Jew stuff. Loud, garish Jew stuff and she detested it.

She was an anti-Semite. It's true. She was just as Jewish as the rest of us, mind—only not. Not in her own imagination anyway. For one thing, she had some Austrian blood. I'm not sure how much, but enough, I guess, to give her bragging rights over Ashkenazi or Eastern European Jews who are traditionally regarded as lower class by the upper-class Germans and Austrians. Her uncle—her mother's brother—was actually named Adolf! He went missing in action fighting for the Austrian empire in World War I. When Hitler rose to power in the thirties, my Ashkenazi grandfather is said to have remarked, "Well, I guess now we know what happened to Adolf." Still, Mom was very proud her family had given one up for the Fatherland.

That—the Austrian line—was on her mother's side. Mom's mother was a very impressive figure apparently, a real hard case. Escaped from Europe with her younger siblings hidden in a haycart, as I recall the tale—escaped not from government oppression, either, but from an evil stepmother who abused and beat her. She was only thirteen years old. She came to America where she grew up to become a radical socialist, a feminist, and an atheist. She divorced her first husband and left their son in his custody. She became a chiropodist, a rare professional woman. She was said to have once performed a do-it-yourself abortion by flinging herself down a flight of stairs. So yeah, a hard case, no doubt about it.

Mom's big sister, my aunt, was a gifted scholar. That won their mother's affection. But my mom was a different matter entirely. Mom's mother dismissed her as a girly flibbertigibbet. "She had no time for me," Mom would say. "But my father liked me because I was pretty."

She *was* pretty too. In her youth, she looked something like those movie stars she admired so much. So whatever parental affection my mother got, it came from her father, who liked a girly flibbertigibbet just fine. Gammy, we boys called him. I knew him only as an old man and can barely remember him. But in his heyday, he was apparently quite dashing and a bit of a rascal. Whenever she got in trouble in school, my mother said, Gammy would come and charm the female teacher and all would be forgiven. He was handsome, big, and athletic. He put himself through college on a basketball scholarship. I've seen his photograph in a book about Jewish American athletes. It was very rare stuff for a Jew of his time.

He became a lawyer but was caught up in one of the reformist sweeps of late-1920s New York City. He was disbarred when he failed to show up in court to face charges of ambulance chasing. He had given a business card to the parents of a boy who'd been in a bicycle accident, something like that. His disgrace was a great source of pain and shame to my mother. She never even told us about it until the old man died, and then she only told my older brother and me. He and I were teenagers then. We thought it was amusing and cool to have a criminal in the family. It suited our roguish sense of ourselves. But it had clearly been traumatic for Mom. After his disbarment, Gammy was employed only sporadically and my mother's family was often broke. Throughout the Great Depression, they were forced to move from place to place whenever they couldn't come up with the rent. They bounced around New York first, and later through Baltimore and its suburbs.

And each time they moved, so my mother told us—and told us proudly too!—before they moved, her father would scan the local phone books to make sure there were no Jewish names near their new location. Gammy didn't want to live in a neighborhood with other Jews.

I don't think he was in denial about who or what he was. A family legend says he once attended a Labor Day parade in Manhattan where a cadre of Hassids were marching along with the rest. Hassids—those are the Orthodox Jews who dress in black and leave their beards and sidelocks unshaven. A couple of thugs on the sidelines started jeering the Jews. Gammy grabbed the punks by their collars, one in each of his big, b-baller hands. He lifted them off their feet, drew their faces close to his, and said through gritted teeth, "Your Lord looked like that, you know." Then he set them down again, silenced.

But he was . . . an ardent assimilationist, I guess you could say. An immigrant, he was proud he had no trace of a greenhorn accent. Proud of his smooth, non-Jewish-seeming features. Proud to have nothing to do with his religion. Proud to go where other Jews could not. When my father arrived to pick up my mother for their first date, he was appalled to find her family living in a house outside of Baltimore across the street from a sign that said "Restricted Neighborhood," meaning *No Jews Allowed. "What on earth are you doing here?"* Dad said to her.

Gammy's antipathies took hold in his younger daughter, his favorite. Like him, she was elegant, charming, and urbane. Like him, she wanted nothing to do with Old World behaviors. The more traditional forms of the Jewish religion were anathema to her. When my parents were married, the traditionalist side of my father's family insisted my mother take a *mikvah* before the wedding. It's a ritual Jewish bath for brides. It involves getting naked while other women wash you. My mother had never heard of the practice and—well!—she thought it absolutely barbaric. She flatly refused to have anything to do with such a thing. There is an entire wing of my extended family that apparently includes famous rabbis and Jewish theologians, but I've never met any of them because they never forgave my mother for blowing off the bath. They never spoke to us after that day.

It wasn't the religion that bothered her most, though. She

could live with that. It was the cultural lines she wouldn't cross. The *mikvah* did not offend her spiritual sense. It just struck her as *uncivilized*, that's all. A civilized person takes her baths in private, thank you very much. A civilized, British-style person doesn't speak some guttural hodge-podge language like Yiddish. I can honestly say, with no exaggeration whatsoever, I've learned more Yiddish words from my WASP-Irish-American wife than I ever learned from Mom. Likewise, any suggestion she was behaving like a clichéd "Jewish mother"—overbearing, smothering, manipulative—made her bridle. In all fairness, she was not that way. She was, rather, aloof and guarded. Hurt in youth and fearful, she lived at some inner distance from the surface of the world.

There is one incident, one exchange between her and my father, that I remember particularly. I must have been no more than four or five at the time, but it struck me even then and stays with me still.

My father, as I've said, was a master of accents and dialects. He could speak gibberish Italian to an Italian and convince the man he was speaking his native tongue. On his radio show every morning, he would pretend to be various characters with various funny voices. His straight man partner, Dee Finch, would interview these make-believe people about the weather or the news or whatever product was being advertised. The radio team—Klavan and Finch—had a little rolling closet in their studio in which they kept a collection of sound props: a guitar, a tambourine, a squeezy car horn that went *aruga* and so on.

But the central prop was the closet door itself. My father would snap the door open and fling it shut—*bang*—to indicate to the listening audience that a new "person" had entered the room. Then he would launch into one of his character voices. There was Trevor Traffic, who would read the traffic report while my father rolled a marble around in an empty can to make it sound as if he were in a helicopter above the highways. There was the doctor Sy Kology, the poet Victor Verse, the Italian singer Emilio Percolator, and so on. All of them were admirably complete creations with their own personalities, accents, and ethnicities.

Among the most popular of this imaginary crowd was Mr. Nat. He was an enthusiastic but hapless middle-manager with some hilariously meaningless title like "Coordinator of Interrelations." I think he represented my father's hostility toward the radio station's various corporate suits who thought they should have some say in the content of his show. Nat would come sailing through the prop door calling out his catchphrase, "Mr. Nat is here!" And you could hear immediately that he had a thick Jewish accent. He sounded like the Brooklyn-born son of Jewish immigrants from Eastern Europe.

The audience loved Nat. What New Yorker didn't have some corporate clown like this in his life? One time when I was suffering from food poisoning, my father took me to the local emergency room. There was a man there who had had a heart attack, a bad one by the looks of it. He was lying on a gurney, near death to all appearances. He recognized my father. He was a listener, a fan. As a nurse arrived with no small sense of urgency to roll him off to the OR, the poor guy managed to lift his hand to Dad in a weak greeting. He drew the oxygen mask down from his face and whispered faintly, "Mr. Nat is here!" and was then wheeled away to what fate God only knows.

My father's show played on the kitchen radio in my house every morning. We heard his voice in the background all through breakfast. My mother went on listening until the show was over at ten o'clock. Often, Dad came home right afterward, in the middle of the day. If he had done some routine he was particularly proud of, he might ask my mother whether she had heard it and if it made her laugh.

This one time he came in, I was playing on the yellow linoleum kitchen floor. My mother was standing at the sink washing dishes. I know how old I was because I was playing with a figure of the One-Eyed, One-Horned, Flyin' Purple People Eater, a character from a novelty song of the late 1950s. The song's producers had given the toy to my father in hopes he would promote the song on his show. My father had passed it along to me.

On his show that morning, my father had apparently done a Mr. Nat sketch that he thought was particularly clever. He asked my mother if she had heard it.

Over the water running into the sink, I heard Mom murmur softly, almost to herself, "I wish you wouldn't do that character."

She did not say this angrily or harshly, not at all. She said it the way any affectionate wife might mention a basically harmless husbandly habit that annoyed or embarrassed her. "I wish you wouldn't laugh so loudly when we're in a nice restaurant, dear." But it immediately set off an alarm bell in attentive little me, which says something in itself. "Why not, Mommy? What's wrong with Mr. Nat? Why shouldn't Daddy do Mr. Nat?" No satisfactory explanation was forthcoming. But I think I suspected the truth even then.

It was because Mr. Nat was a Jew. Not just a Jew, a rambunctious, lower-class, Old-World Ashkenazi Jew. It was too close to her inner reality, too threatening to her aspirations. She wanted no stain of that sort of Jewish identity on her or on us.

I must have known that, sensed it, even as a child. I think it must have colored everything.

CHAPTER 2

ADDICTED TO DREAMS

I was an unhappy little boy and I escaped into daydreams.

In these dreams, I was a hero who rescued girls from danger. I was a cowboy about to step into a gunfight to save a widow's farm, or a soldier battling Nazis to reach the French mademoiselle in her cottage behind enemy lines. Sometimes I was like one of the superheroes from the comic books I loved. Elementary School Kid was just my secret identity. No one knew that I could become invisible, or shrink to the size of an atom, or breathe under water, or run at the speed of light. Or, best of all, that I could fly: fly anywhere and drop from the sky like heaven's vengeance—through the window, shattering glass—into the dark city alley where the henchmen lurked or anywhere else where girls were in danger and could be rescued in the nick of time.

There were other dreams, too, more personal, more specific dreams that weren't inspired by comic books or television or movies but that grew organically out of my own childhood hurts and yearnings. I wanted to be a scientist, an inventor like my hero Thomas Edison. I had read every book in the school library about Edison. He had been thrashed by his father as I had been, humiliated and ridiculed by his father as I was now. And yet he had grown up to daydream the modern world into existence one gadget at a time—stock ticker, phonograph, movie camera—one idea after another going on in his head like a lightbulb (lightbulb!).

In my dreams, I invented . . . something. I could never really think of anything exciting to invent, even in my dreams, which probably should have served as a warning that I was going to have to find a different profession in real life. But in my dreams, I had invented something or other and had thus become the world's first famous Kid Scientist. A grateful nation awarded me my own astronomical observatory plus a special miniature car I could drive around town on my own. I was given my own house, too, in which I could live separate from my family with one of the girls I had a crush on in school or, better yet, a girl I imagined, a girl of my dreams.

I don't suppose these fantasies were much different in kind from the fantasies of other boys. We all played at being heroes: cowboys, soldiers, supermen, knights in armor, or a secret gang of good-guy thieves. In the acre and half-acre yards behind our plush and placid suburban houses, beneath the tall oaks and maples and hickories, and on the ridges of gently rolling hills, we acted out the courage of mighty men of valor, staging duels with sticks for swords, donning plastic army helmets and toystore cowboy hats and dodging in and out among the tree trunks and bushes, shooting at each other with make-believe guns.

The sports we played were also a kind of heroic daydream. All spring long, in the hours between the end of school and twilight, on placid streets of quiet homes where cars passed only rarely, where girls jumped rope and played hopscotch on the sidewalks, while moms made dinner and kept an eye on us through the kitchen windows, we concocted a million variations of baseball. Fungo, stickball, Wiffle ball, catch—or just bouncing a tennis ball off the garage door. In the autumn, we played football, two-handed touch. Or sometimes, one of us would take his bike to the top of our street and ride down the hill no-handed, shouting, "It's Pile On time!" Six, eight, ten, or twelve boys would come running eagerly out of their houses to gather in the Klavan backyard. Someone would place a football on the grass in the center of the pack. And at the starting shout—"Pile on!"—we'd pile on, every man for himself, a brutal and uproarious scrum. The radio announcers in our heads described the action for the fans at home, and the crowds in our imaginations went wild.

We were heroes even in our quiet hours, playing board games that cast us as generals fighting for world domination or detectives solving murders or just masterminds locked in a raw battle of wits. I loved—still love—all kinds of games and puzzles. I was so good at checkers for a while that even my older brother had to turn over the board sometimes to keep me from winning. At night I would lie awake and imagine games that would play automatically, machines that would fight whole battles for you while you worked the controls. If there had been video games when I was a child, I would have grown up without ever seeing the light of day.

Instead of video games, we had playsets: collections of figures and accessories. You moved them around with your hands while whispering dialogue and sound effects under your breath. There were Civil War playsets with the soldiers colored blue and gray; Revolutionary War sets with the British red from head to toe; and Fort Apache, in which the US Cavalry, all blue, fought off the Injuns, all brown. I even had an *Untouchables* set in which federal agents traded bullets with scar-faced gangsters on the rooftops of a toy Chicago. *Rat-ta-tat-tat.* The plastic gangsters, still clutching the tommy guns molded into their arms, would somersault, screaming to their bloody deaths on the pavement below.

It was all a kind of dreaming, a way to bring some sense of hazard and nobility into our grassy, safe, and well-looked-after world. Boys are born yearning for battle and adventure. And our fathers' lives had given that longing a shape and a name: the shape and name of war. Our dads had fought in World War II. My own dad had been stationed at an airfield on the island of Guam in the Pacific. He told us stories. About how he'd seen the semiliquid remains of fliers scraped out of cockpits with a shovel. About how he'd heard snipers in the jungle at night. About how he sank in mud up to his backside out there.

A lot of our dads told such stories. And we could see their adventures for ourselves in old movies on TV and sometimes even in new movies in the theaters. *Sands of Iwo Jima. Merrill's Marauders. The Longest Day.* It was all very cool and very frightening. We asked our mothers: Would we have to go to a war when we grew up? And we wondered to ourselves: Would we rise to the occasion? Would we be heroes like our fathers were? Or would we fail the test, and fall prey to the fears we felt deep down even as we played at being brave?

Our mothers assured us there would be no more armies when we grew up, and no more wars. But we weren't convinced. We knew the Russians were out there, bad guys who did not believe in freedom and wanted to take over the world. Sometimes at school we had air-raid drills in which we practiced hiding under our desks so we'd be ready in case the Reds dropped the atom bomb on us. Our schoolhouse was a one-story, gray-clapboard building on the crest of a hill of grass. The southern wall of my classroom had a line of windows looking out on the tree-shaded street below. The school principal warned us that if an atom bomb struck, the window glass would shatter and shards would go flying. I imagined I would have to crawl on my belly like an infantryman to avoid being cut to pieces by the glittering barrage as I rescued the girls.

We were boys in a place of safety in a world of danger and we dreamed.

But if my dreams were no different in kind than the dreams of other boys, they were different in degree. I dreamed without ceasing, obsessively. I had a rule that my dreams had to make sense. That is, the stories in them needed to be held together by some sort of internal logic. It wasn't that my fantasies had to be realistic. I could fly in them; I could drive around town in a child-sized car; I could suddenly be a cowboy—all that was okay. But there had to be a narrative built into the daydream explaining how such things could have come to be; a backstory, as they call it in the movie business nowadays.

Could I fly because I came from another planet, or had some special potion done the trick? Had the grown-ups met to rewrite the laws in order to allow a child prodigy such as myself to own a car? Was I a cowboy because I had been born in an alternative universe, or had I traveled back in time from the modern world? I labored at these explanations diligently, even when it became a tiresome chore. I was not satisfied until my fantasies *worked*. Only then would they become part of my library of dreams.

I shaped and reshaped these dreams whenever I was alone, and sometimes—more and more often as the years went by—I sought out solitude so I could go on dreaming. If you had asked me why I dreamed so much, what reality I was escaping from, I don't think I would have been able to tell you. I thought I lived a happy life. I thought my family was the best family ever. My father's bristling anger and the way he ridiculed me, my mother's weird dissociation, the sadistic violence that sometimes erupted among my three brothers and me were all enacted within a context of genuine affection and suburban normalcy. I did not see that they were there. I did not know they were making me unhappy. But more and more, I daydreamed to escape them, and then even more and more.

My walk to school in the morning was my favorite time to

drift into fantasy. It was a journey of maybe a third of a mile, a fifteen-minute walk for a six-, seven-, or eight-year-old child.

We lived in the last house but one on Old Colony Lane. It was a hill on which the houses got smaller and smaller as you came down. There were porticoed white mansions perched up at the top. Then, mid-slope, there were fine, stately homes. By the time you got down to the bottom where we were, the living was relatively modest. Our own house grew larger over time as my father prospered and added rooms and bought the neighbor's backyard to add to ours. But at the start, it was just a smallish colonial, white clapboards and green shutters, with a narrow front lawn.

It was only a minute's walk from my front door to the end of the road. From there you could either turn right onto the wide, bright, open path of Chadwick Road, or go straight ahead. Ahead lay the junction of Andover and Plymouth. It was a strangely dark corner. An empty house hunkered in mossy shadows under a dense cluster of oaks and pines. We made a haunted mansion out of it, of course. My big brother and his friends hung hangmen's nooses from the tree branches to frighten us. They cut out cardboard hands and streaked them with blood-red marker and stuck them in the earth so it looked as if dead men were digging out of their graves.[1]

But while going by the ghost house did send a chill through me, I opted for that route most often. There were fewer kids along the way. If I left home five minutes early, I could avoid running into my pal from up the block. Then I could walk to school alone, and I could dream uninterrupted.

Books tucked under my arm, I ambled along the morning streets imagining stories, lost in stories. It was not an empty state of mind. It was a positive pleasure, like going to the movies or watching TV. I looked forward to it. I enjoyed it. I still remember the melancholy that would come over me as the little gray schoolhouse came into sight and the end of the walk drew near. I was sorry that my best time for dreaming was almost over.

Not that school put an end to my dreaming. No, no, I dreamed all through it. I was a terrible student. I managed to get top grades in every subject except handwriting (mine was then, as it is now, illegible), but it was all fraud. I could read well and write well and talk glibly and even figure out math problems in my head. So I could bluff my way through subjects I knew nothing about, and neither my teachers nor my parents, nor even my friends, were aware that I was hardly doing any schoolwork at all. I would come home every afternoon and dump my books on the table in the front hall. I would tell my mother I had finished my homework at lunchtime or in study period. Then, after a snack of cookies and milk, I would rush out of the house again, jump on my bike, and pedal off in search of other kids to play with. I learned nothing. I knew nothing: no historical facts, no mathematical formulas, no passages from the books we were supposed to have read.

As a result, my time in the classroom was divided between boredom and terror. I would sit dazed in a fog of immovable minutes and hours. With some lesson or other droning on in the background, I would doodle jets and monsters in my notebook. I'd imagine Russian soldiers kicking in the door and how I'd fight my way through rifle fire to rescue the fascinatingly pale girl who sat in the front row where she was forever eagerly raising her hand. Then, every now and again, the fog would suddenly be split by a blue-electric flash of fear. The teacher had asked a question! Now she was scanning the children's faces, face by face, searching for someone to call on. It was an easy question too. Anyone who had even glanced at the reading would know the answer. But I had not, and I did not.

The suspense was agony. The fear of public humiliation— dreadful: the fear that my charade would be undone, my ignorance exposed for all the world to see. All my dreams of epic heroism would evaporate on the instant and I would be forced to stutter and sweat through some mealy-mouthed excuse that everyone would know was a lie. I waited, breathless, for the teacher to decide.

In the event, the catastrophe rarely struck. I generally made such a convincing show of being smart that it never occurred to my teachers what an ignoramus I really was; it never occurred to them to test me. The axe almost always fell on some other poor shnook with lower grades and a worse reputation. From him who has not, even what he has shall be taken away.

But though one unbearable moment of suspense might have passed, I knew there'd be another one coming and soon. As I grew in ignorance, my fear of exposure began to haunt even my off-hours. Increasingly, my afternoons and nights and weekends became poisoned with a pervasive nausea of anxiety. I soothed myself with daydreaming and play, so that I neglected my homework even more and had to worry even more about being found out.

Dreams and anxiety: they fed on each other. The dreams—my heroism and courage and genius in the dreams—created an image of myself that I felt I had to live up to, or try to live up to, or appear to live up to at least. I couldn't stand the idea of being exposed as weak or cowardly or stupid. It was strange really, when you think about it. In some ways, I was such a little conman. But at the same time I seemed to be nurturing the first small glimmerings of what might one day become a sense of integrity. I wanted to be what I pretended to be. I wanted to be what I dreamed.

That was why, or one of the reasons why, I got into so many fistfights. A lot of fistfights, all through elementary school and into junior high. It didn't occur to me until much later how bizarre it was that I should have fought so much. I lived in an affluent Long Island suburb of Manhattan. I wasn't a roughneck. It wasn't a roughneck town. And yet I always seemed to be slugging it out with somebody, and often it was somebody who was a lot bigger than I was. Sometimes I was in the right and sometimes in the wrong and sometimes there wasn't much to choose between one argument and the other. Once or twice, I was the aggressor and a bully, occasions that make me ashamed to this day. But more often than not, I was just standing my ground in a situation where another boy would have yielded to the intractable boy logic of big and small. Some older kids would try to chase me off a field and I wouldn't go. Or one of the school thugs would pick on a little kid or on a girl and I'd step in. Sometimes I got beaten up. Sometimes I dusted the guy. A lot of times it ended with nothing more than some big talk and posturing. But because of my dreams, because I had to live up to the image of myself in my dreams, I could never back down or run away. And if another kid and I agreed to meet somewhere after school and punch out our differences, I could never fail to keep the appointment. I had to be there.

By the time I was in fifth grade, my reputation was such that when my teachers sent a really bad kid to the principal's office for discipline, they would assign me to escort him, my hand on his elbow, as if I were the law of the land. One of these tough guys once elbowed me in the stomach and ran for it, trying to escape. I had to chase him across the playground and tackle him. It was like a scene out of a cop movie—except we were ten years old!

I remember a touch football game I played in summer camp once. I was on the line. A much older boy, fifteen or sixteen at least, a head taller than I was and a real muscle man, was positioned opposite me. Each time the ball was snapped, the kid would run straight into me, smack me around, trample me. It was not the usual touch football roughhousing. It was elbows to the face and fists to the stomach and when he knocked me over he'd step on me where I lay. I told him to cut it out. He refused. I complained to the ref. But the thug wouldn't listen to the ref either. Pretty soon, I was crying. Blood and snot were running down my face. The ref told me to line up somewhere else, but I wouldn't do it. A teammate pulled me aside and told me we'd get revenge later. We'd put something slimy in the guy's bed at night. I wouldn't do it. I purposely placed myself smack in front of the thug every play. Every play, he came barreling into me, hell bent on destruction. Crying, bleeding, drooling blood, I went back to the line. I made the thug run over me again and then again. I made him elbow me again in my streaked and grimy face. I made him kick me when I was down again and then I got up for the next play, and, again, I lined up in front of him.

I wore him out. I wore him down to the level of his conscience, even his. Toward the end of the game, he stopped throwing elbows. He stopped knocking me over. Finally, *he* started to avoid *me*, to move *his* position, and to run around me whenever he could. When I'd plant myself in front of him, he wouldn't meet my eyes. He'd attack the guy next to me or he'd go after the ball carrier as he was supposed to. When the game was over, he approached me. He squeezed my shoulder with his hand. He told me I was a tough little guy. I sneered at him. I didn't care what he thought. I despised him. But I felt I'd beaten him in the only way I could.

It was because of my dreams. It was because I was a hero in my daydreams, and I wanted to be what I pretended to be. "In dreams begin responsibilities," as the poet Yeats said, and the responsibility not to fall short of my own illusions weighed on me constantly. My fantastic self-image rode on my shoulders, a burden that only added to my general feeling of dread. It is not fun to get punched. It is the opposite of fun. When you have been punched, you do not want to be punched again, not ever. I haven't been in a fistfight for more than forty years, and yet people who have been in fistfights, people who have punched people and been punched, read the fight scenes in my novels and say to me, "You've been in fistfights too. You've punched people and have been punched too." It's not an experience you forget. The fights and the threat of fighting and the appointments to fight and waiting to keep the appointments—all of it was a source of anxiety for me. And to escape that anxiety, I dreamed.

I dreamed away long hours of every day. At night in bed, before I went to sleep, I would review my collection of completed dreams, the ones that didn't need any more work, the ones that made sense and were ready to be imagined. I would picture a strip of movie film, complete with sprockets. I would picture it running frame by frame through a viewer, the sort of hand-cranked viewer my dad had in his basement darkroom. On each frame of the film strip there would be a picture of a dream, a different picture, a different dream on each—atom man, boy genius, cowboy, whatever. I would select one and close my eyes and the story would begin to play out in my mind. The dream would soothe me and relax me like reading a book until finally I could sleep.

All that dreaming and making dreams: it was good practice for a someday novelist, I guess, especially a novelist of adventure and suspense. But it wasn't a very healthy way to spend a boyhood. Even I knew that, or came to realize it after a while. I was dreaming more and more and becoming less and less aware of the reality around me. I was seven or eight years old, and I was losing the knack for direct experience. I could feel the tactile sense of the world's immediacy slipping from my fingertips. I could see the light of the present moment dimming into darkness.

If TV sitcoms idealized the American suburbs of the 1960s, the works of the artistic elite disparaged them ceaselessly, then and now. The songs of Pete Seeger, novels like *Revolutionary Road*, the stories of John Cheever, movies like *Pleasantville* and *American Beauty*, television series like *Mad Men*: in all of them, that long-ago land of lawns and houses is depicted as a country of stultifying conformity and cultural emptiness, sexual hypocrisy, alcoholism, and spiritual despair. Privilege murders the senses there, the creatives tell us. Gender roles strangle freedom. Family life turns the heart of adventure to ashes. There's bigotry and gossip and dangerous liaisons behind every closed door. Oh, the soul, the human soul! In the suburbs of fiction, she is forever dying.

But me, I kind of liked it there. As a little boy anyway. What was wrong with it? You had your trees, you had your sidewalks, you had your birds and squirrels and moms and dads. Kids played in the street through the afternoons and went home past warmly lighted windows in the evenings. There were summer barbecues and baseball games. There were high piles of autumn leaves that you could hurl yourself into. In winter, there were snows so deep you could dig long tunnels underneath the drifts. In spring, there was a flavor to the air that made you yearn for you-didn't-know-what. If the suburban ideal of the sitcom was false, so are the elite attacks on a way of life that most citizens of the earth would have sold their souls for. Were people miserable there? Maybe, but the truth is people can be miserable anywhere. You can find hypocrites, drunks, and adulterers anywhere you find humanity. Why not live somewhere with some peace and quiet and open spaces and a twenty-minute commute to the city?

But this world—this suburban world I really did love, this world for which I felt a sentimental, almost nostalgic, affection even as a child—it was sinking away from me, sinking to the bottom of a sea of dreams, visible now only distantly through the wavery undercurrent. I would walk to school and find when I arrived that I could remember not one moment of the journey, not one piece of scenery, not one face or car or incident, only my dreams. I would take long bike rides and come to myself on some strange road, hardly knowing how I got there. Even during games, even during conversations, I would sometimes mentally absent myself to go on some imagined adventure, and come back only half aware of what we had been doing or saying while my mind was gone.

I hardly even saw the trees anymore. I had always—have always—had a sort of mystic fondness for trees. To this day, my mind is nowhere more at peace than in a forest. As a boy, I would lie under this one particular maple in our backyard. I would lace my fingers behind my head and watch the pattern of leaves against the sky. It was one of my favorite pastimes, no kidding. There was an apple tree I liked to climb in our front yard near the street. I would hide in the branches for hours sometimes, watching people pass and cars go by. The autumn change of colors all over town, the whisper of breezes in high parkland pines, the weirdness of weeping willows at the roadside, the boy squirrels chasing girl squirrels up the trunks of oaks in crazy spirals like squirrels in a cartoon, the rare scarlet cardinal meditating in the deep foliage. As an aspiring tough guy, I was embarrassed by how much these things delighted me. They were secret pleasures I did not discuss with anyone.

But over time I found that, whenever I was among the trees, I wasn't really there at all anymore; I was dreaming. I would make special trips to the backyard to lie beneath the maple. I would try to recapture the sensation of watching its branches against the sky. I would try to concentrate on the patterns and colors that had once fascinated me. But my mind would drift away into dreams.

It bothered me. I missed the trees. I missed the walk to school. I missed my friends and my games and the weather and the whole wide world—not just the facts of them but the presence and awareness of them, the being there with them. It was all dreams for me now. Nothing but dreams.

I had reached that stage in an addiction when you notice that the pleasure of the thing is gone. You didn't really want that last cigarette or drink. You didn't really enjoy it. You just had to have it. With me, the boy me, it was fantasy. Fantasy like mist—mist like ivy—twining around me, enclosing me. I didn't like it anymore. I just couldn't make it stop.

So I did what most addicts do at that juncture. I resolved to break the habit. From now on, I decided, I was going to *pay attention.* Maybe not to everything, maybe not all the time. I would begin with something small, something manageable. The walk to school, say. Yes, that would do it. I would pay full attention during the walk to school. No more daydreams. I would focus on what I saw. I would listen to the sounds—the birds, the breezes, the passing cars. I would smell the air. I would live in the experience of the moment.

I was eight years old.

I began the project on a Monday morning in autumn. I banged through the front-door screen with my books beneath my arm and marched off to school resolutely alert.

Now, anyone who has ever practiced any of the Eastern-style mindfulness techniques, zen or yoga or tai chi or suchlike, knows just how incredibly difficult it is to do what I was trying to do. To be aware, to be present in the moment, to silence your own interior jibbering and face life naked-minded is, as I would later learn, the entire goal of some spiritual enterprises, the very essence of enlightenment. No wonder too. It's hard. Most of the time we can't even unglue our noses from our screens and devices long enough to pay attention to our internal dialogue, let alone break out of that dialogue into pure existence. Try it. Try it for sixty seconds. Complete inner silence. Not one word of thought. Utter awareness. It's hard.

But I tried. I walked along. I focused diligently on the tremulous green lobes of the neighbor's pachysandra. I wondered if I'd forgotten to bring my math book. No, I had it. Now where was I? Back to awareness. The lofty clouds billowing over the sky above the ghost house. Would there be kickball at recess? I liked kickball. I could see myself sending a solid shot over the heads of the outfielders. No, no, that's no good. Focus, focus. Look at the texture of the Macadam where it meets the stone curb. Ah, now, I'm doing it! My mind is clear. That's amazing! It's as if I've invented a whole new way of thinking. I'll become the first truly enlightened child. Aliens will come to earth searching for our wisest human and discover, through their advanced brain scans, that it's me. They'll implant their alien powers in me, powers that will allow me to govern the world. With my mind so clear, so focused, I'll be able to use those powers more wisely even than the president . . .

And then I was at school and could not remember how I had gotten there.

Total failure. I'd hardly paid attention for more than a consecutive couple of seconds before the dreams overtook me. But I was not yet discouraged. I tried again a second day. Again, I couldn't get more than three or four steps before my concentration was broken by a random thought and the thought became a chain and the chain became a dream and I was gone, gone, gone.

It was dispiriting. It was even disturbing. Was my whole life going to be strangled by a clinging ivy-mist of dreams?

Then, on the third day: a breakthrough.

I was walking on the longest straightaway of the journey, the stretch of Piccadilly Road that ran from the ghost house to where you turned up Devon to the school. I was passing lawn after sloping lawn and leaf-hidden home after home, psychically trying to claw the tendrils of fantasy from my mind so I could see clearly. There'd be moments of awareness, seconds of naked reality. And then a drifting thought. And the tendrils would twine back around me, thicker than before.

I was about two-thirds of the way to the corner, almost out of time, frustrated to the point where I was beginning to consider abandoning the entire experiment. Then suddenly I spotted a high tree branch off in the distance against the backdrop of the September sky.

I don't know what it was about that branch that caught my full attention. Something, though, because I can remember the look of it to this day. It was the branch of an oak tree, I think. Far off, in the backyard not of the house right in front of me, but of the house behind that one. It was a single branch jutting out two or three feet beyond the tree's green crown, near the top. The stouter part of it was bare, colored that white-brown-gray branch color there's no good name for. (Who ever says "taupe"?) But there was a cluster of dark green leaves near the tip of it, where the main arm forked into dwindling twiglets. The sky behind the leaves was very blue with a single small, white cumulus cloud slowly drifting through it.

And I saw it, really saw it. The branch, the sky, the cloud, the whole scene. I broke through my thoughts and my dreams and myself and I was just there, completely there. I stopped walking. I stood with my schoolbooks held low against my leg. The cooly yearning autumn breeze stroked my cheeks and stirred my hair and I gazed at that branch and my mind was silent. My attention was turned completely outward. No fantasy, only the world. I saw it all.

What a disappointment it was! There was nothing to it. It was just a branch, that's all. Real enough but cold, empty of emotional presence. It held no sweetness, no pleasure, no beauty. It was not like the high branches of my backyard oak when I lay under it, or the branches of my apple tree when I climbed on them and hid among them. I was fond of those; I loved them. This—this faraway branch—it was just a fact. A lifeless pattern. A branch against the sky, some leaves, a drifting cloud. This wasn't what I had been looking for at all. This was nothing. A branch. A cloud. The sky. Nothing.

I came back into myself, let down, deflated. I understood at once what had gone wrong, the flaw at the heart of my whole experiment. I don't remember now what eight-year-old words I used to describe my understanding to myself, but the gist of it was this: The world had no beauty of its own. The beauty of the world was created in the human experience, in me. The very fact of beauty, the very idea that something could be beautiful, only existed in me. The point was not to see the world. There was nothing out there to see, nothing worthwhile at any rate, just shapes, just patterns. The point was to *experience* the world, to know it simultaneously both without and within.

But I had lost the talent for living like that, and I could not get it back again merely by staring.

How then? How could I reclaim the world and my life in the world? How could a person free himself from the prison of his own consciousness in order to know the beauty of the world as it existed only within his consciousness?

Ah, well—that was a puzzle way beyond the abilities of an eight-year-old, even a puzzle-loving eight-year-old like me.

And so I left the branch behind. I left the world behind. I went on my way to school, that day and all the days that followed, in solitude, cut off from reality, surrendered to stories, addicted to dreams.

CHAPTER 3

BAR MITZVAH BOY

There were three main synagogues in our town, as I remember it. Each represented a different degree of religious observance, light, medium, or heavy: Reform, Conservative, or Orthodox. We were Conservative by my dad's decree. We had a Seder meal at Passover. We went to synagogue on Rosh Hashanah, the Jewish New Year. We lit candles on the eight nights of Hanukkah. We even fasted on Yom Kippur, the annual Day of Atonement. We went to Hebrew School, too, twice during the week, I think it was, and maybe a third time on Sundays. There we were supposed to learn Hebrew and the Bible and ultimately prepare for our bar mitzvahs.

My mom helped out with all this, of course. She prepared the meals, chauffeured us to temple, and so on. But she made it clear she was only doing her duty by my dad. She would tease him about it. She would say, "You know you're just doing this to please your dead father." My paternal grandfather died when I was very young. My clearest memory of him was of seeing him close to the end of his life. "Prepare yourself," my father had told me and my older brother as we climbed the narrow stairs to his apartment. "He doesn't look good."

I remember a shockingly withered and gentle creature swamped by the wing chair from which he could no longer rise. In his youth, however, he was a stern and intimidating traditionalist apparently, a tough-guy pawnbroker who kept a kosher house and expected his two sons to do the same. My mother felt Dad maintained Jewish practices in our house only for fear of his memory.

My dad acknowledged—ruefully—that there was some truth to that. But our Hebrew rituals and schooling were important to him personally too. He saw the world as a gentile world forever hostile to its Jews. He didn't want us to retreat an inch in the face of its bigotry. *They'll still kill you, even if you try to pretend to be one of them, so don't humiliate yourself with cultural surrender.* That was the general idea.

But also, and more reasonably, there was this. My father wanted us, his sons, to know our own people. He wanted us to take their history seriously. He didn't want us to leave our heritage behind.

Which was fair enough, in theory. But in practice, there was a problem with it, a big problem with all of it—with the high holy days and the Hebrew School and the bar mitzvahs—one big problem that troubled my heart from an early age. My parents did not believe in God.

My mother, for her part, was a stone atheist, like her

mother before her. I've never met anyone else as firm as she was in her disbelief. Oh, sometimes she would make some vague gesture toward the idea of a deity. She felt it was her duty as a mother, I think. She didn't want to pull the metaphysical rug out from under her children's feet too abruptly lest they bruise themselves plummeting into the existential abyss. She'd tell us things like: *God is the people who love you.* Or: *There's something out there; no one knows what for sure.* But, of course, you can't fool kids with that sort of mealymouthed malarkey. I knew where she stood. As I got older, I could even coax her true opinion out of her from time to time. *If you ask me, it's all a lot of hooey.*

Of my father's beliefs, I'm not quite as sure. He was close and canny about them, not just with us but with himself as well, I think; maybe even with God. It was not in his nature to openly defy a Gigantic Invisible Jew who could give you cancer just by thinking about it. But by the same token, he wasn't simply going to kowtow to the Power. He felt the need to give the Lord a little *zetz* from time to time—a Yiddish smack—of sarcasm, disrespect, and disbelief. I think he prayed when things troubled him; it couldn't hurt. The father he appeased with his observances was sometimes his own father and sometimes the Big Father in the Sky. He hedged his bets: he took Pascal's Wager but held half of his cash in reserve in case the game turned out to be some kind of cheap hustle.

In any case, for child me, the larger point was this: God was not a living presence in my home. We did not say grace before meals. We did not kneel down by our beds at night.

We were not told to pray in times of hardship. We were not referred to the will of God in matters of morality. Aside from collecting pennies for UNICEF on Halloween and occasionally putting quarters aside for the United Jewish Appeal, we did no volunteer work and had no charity life of any kind.

For me, this rendered our Jewish observances absurd. I was the boy, after all, who demanded that even his daydreams make some kind of sense. I became frustrated with a mystery story if even a single thread of the plot was left loose. And I had what I would call a very *Jewish* insistence on the rational basis for any supernatural belief. I could see that the magnificent four-thousand-year-old structure of Jewish theology and tradition was, at its core, a kind of language for communicating with the divine presence. Subtract the Almighty and what was the purpose of it? It was just an empty temple, its foundations resting on nothing, its spires pointing only toward the dark.

The absurdity of our godless Judaism affected all the family's practices. My earliest memories of our Passover Seders are uproariously comical. The dinners would begin as carefully orchestrated and solemn religious rituals. Slowly at first, then very quickly, they would devolve into swing-from-the-rafters madcap circuses with my brothers and me clowning around like wild monkeys. A Seder really is a fine event. It's a dignified but joyful remembrance of how God freed the Hebrews from slavery in Egypt. The youngest son asks four prescribed questions of his father so the father can explain the majestic meaning of the feast. The participants drip wine on a plate while intoning the names of the ten plagues with which God crushed the resistance of Pharaoh: *blood . . . frogs . . . lice . . .* Everyone slouches on cushioned chairs to remind themselves that they are free men and women, no longer slaves. It's lovely.

But in my house we added a ritual in which my little brothers half swallowed the silver wine cups and then spat them across the table into each other's foreheads. My older brother, meanwhile, kept up a withering sardonic commentary. And I put my face on the tablecloth and laughed till I wept. My mother would hide her smile at the antic chaos but my father, no. That was another part of our ritual: he would routinely storm out of the room in a fury over our disrespect.

It was shameful, I know. But it really was funny. And how else could it have been? Without God, none of it made any sense. Hebrew School? For me, who already hated ordinary school, an extra classroom hour every few days was suffocating torture. Who were these grave and self-important men who kept us from our games to teach us Hebrew and Torah? Why were they bothering us with such things? With their thick sepulchral accents and their harsh, punitive piety? With their bizarre language and their empty legends of an unknowable past? And Israel! They were forever yammering on about the nation of Israel! I remember when the Israelis, outnumbered and pressed against the sea, defeated the Arab nations in the Six-Day War. The Hebrew School front office piped the news reports into our classrooms over the loudspeakers. Our teachers wept at the miraculous victory. I found it ridiculous. I was American. What was Israel to me and who was I to Israel?

I was somehow managing to shuck and jive my way through ordinary school, but I didn't have the energy or even the common courtesy to fake it here. I was sullen and unresponsive in religious classes. Sharp-tongued and disrespectful to the pompous and overbearing teachers. When we had tests on the Bible, I wrote flippant answers to questions about stories I'd never bothered to read.

How did Moses help Joshua defeat the Amalekites?

He brought the tanks.

Once, to my absolute horror, a session of Hebrew School conflicted with a game of the World Series in which the Yankees were playing. I put a transistor radio in my pants pocket and ran the earplug wire up through the sleeve of my sweater. All through the lesson on Exodus, I sat leaning my head on my hand, pressing the palmed earbud into my ear so I could listen to the game. My father used to say, "You can't flunk out of being Jewish." But man, I tried. I remember more than one report card when I received a P in every single subject. It stood for Poor, the lowest grade you could get.

By the time I began to prepare for my bar mitzvah, I was utterly alienated from the entire enterprise.

"I don't believe in this," I told my father. "I don't want to do it."

"It doesn't matter," he said. "You have to."

Three years later, fueled by seething adolescent rage, I would have defied him. When that time came, I did defy him, again and again. My fury and stubbornness drove him crazy, literally drove him to seek psychiatric help. But at twelve years old, I still thought I lived in the happiest of happy TV-type families. To defy my father in this most basic realm of his authority would have been to pull down the pillars of that illusion like Samson pulled down the pillars in the temple. I didn't have the wherewithal. I complained and protested—often—but I did not resist. And my resentment of the whole process burned like acid in my blood.

Naturally, in a town like Great Neck, bar mitzvahs were a big deal. The thirteen-year-old boy, in his best Saturday suit, would stand with the rabbi and cantor at the front of the synagogue. The pews would be filled with friends and relations from all over. The boy would read out a Torah portion in Hebrew, not spoken but sung to a ritualized Eastern tune that he'd had to memorize line by line. Afterward, he would make a speech, written himself and vetted by the rabbi. "Today I am a man," he would say, affirming that he had now accepted his place as a full-fledged member of the Jewish tribe. Increasingly, in those days, girls did this too: a *bat* mitzvah, it was called. I believe it was just then becoming the fashion.

In any case, boy or girl, the ceremony was generally followed by a massive and elaborate party, comparable in excess to a full-on white wedding reception. A hall was rented, some cavernous place with pink walls and enormous chandeliers and bubbling fountains. Or sometimes, in summer weather, a huge tent was set up in the backyard next to the pool. Indoors or out, a live band would play the new rock 'n' roll music. There would be enough bad food to feed a small nation, oceans of terrible Jewish wine, sentimental congratulatory speeches, and lavish gifts of jewelry and cash. It was a garish business, as we upper-crust Klavans never failed to point out, but it was a happy one too. Most kids looked forward to their big day. My older brother had survived it without too much emotional agony—or so, at least, it seemed to me.

But I hated it, every minute of it. It galled me to my soul. I felt I was being bullied into a public act of hypocrisy. I was being forced to pretend to accept what I did not: Judaism without God, Judaism as a sop to my father's dead father, Judaism as a fist shaken at a gentile world that was just as much my world as the gentiles'. This was the only Judaism I had experienced, and it was foreign and false to me. I wanted no part of it. The idea of lying about that in front of everyone I knew violated something very basic in me.

The preparation for the event was like Hebrew School only ten times worse. Extra classes at night. Extra homework to ignore. Extra humiliation to suffer when I showed up in the extra classes unprepared. Plus, on top of all that, a rabbi actually came to the house once or twice a week. A fat, sweaty, unpleasant man as I recall him. He would later go on to be convicted by a federal jury of being part of a loan-sharking operation in league with some New York mafiosi. I believe he did some serious time upstate.

The rabbi would sit shoulder to shoulder with me upstairs in my room at my desk, our heads bowed together over the open book of Torah. He would cue and harry me through the incomprehensible Hebrew I was supposed to be able to read by then but couldn't. He would sing a line and then I'd sing it back to him and then he'd sing it again and I'd sing back and so on until I had the words and music more or less memorized. Then I was supposed to practice in my spare time. Then he would come back a few days later and we'd review what I'd learned and move on to the next part.

Except, as I need hardly say at this point, I never practiced, never. As the day drew near, I found I barely knew my part at all, just patches of it here and there, and I could sing only a vague meandering imitation of the tune. So, of course, when my bar mitzvah finally arrived, I stepped onto the chancery with the purest sense of dread. It was like one of those nightmares where you find yourself on a Broadway stage but can't remember your lines. There I was in tie and jacket, standing in the temple before a congregation full of family and friends. My pulse was thundering. My spit had first turned sour then gone dry. I joined the rabbi in the sacred procedure of lifting the bejeweled Torah scrolls from their cabinet. We paraded them majestically before the pews. We laid them on the podium—the *bimah*—and rolled them open to the proper place. I took up the Torah pointer—the *yad*, it's called—and placed it under those ancient and noble words that, after years of attending Hebrew School, I could read no better than if they were chicken tracks or a schizophrenic's meaningless doodles. And I began to sing.

Well, the rabbi had come to the house often enough that I had some vague idea of where the words and music were located on the spectrum of available sounds. I found their general location as a man might stumble into the side of his own barn while wandering lost in the dark of night. Since the words meant nothing to me anyway, I only had to imitate the noise of them to get by. And for the most part I did, with the loan-sharking rabbi whispering helpful cues into my ear from time to time. There were a few portions that were lost to my memory completely, but I never faltered for all that. I had inherited a small measure of my father's talent for realistic-sounding foreign-language gibberish. Faced with an absolute mental blank, I invented a bunch of Hebrew-like gobbledy-gook on the spot and pushed through, singing meaningless nonsense without a pause. I don't know how many people noticed. The only person to mention it to me was a cousin of mine, a sophisticated lad a few years older than me. He sidled up to me after the ceremony as I was receiving the kisses and congratulations of my jubilant relatives. "I don't think I've ever heard anyone ad-lib the Torah before," he murmured in my ear. I laughed wildly—with relief but also with a grifter's pleasure at having pulled off a successful con.

I don't remember the party afterward. This strikes me as odd. I was thirteen, after all. It was a big occasion. I should remember. But I don't. I've blocked it out. My conflicting emotions must have overwhelmed me. On the surface, I surely felt happy enough. I'd gotten through the ceremony. There was a party in my honor. Food, music, dancing, gifts. But inwardly, I think I was half insane with rage and shame—more rage and shame than I could feel or know—at having been forced to violate my deepest sense of things.

I do remember this, though: Being a Klavan thing, the

party was supposed to be more tasteful than the usual *nou-veau riche* Great Neck affair. There was no rented hall, no pink walls, no chandeliers, no fountains. We did have a tent in the backyard, but it was just a small one over the badminton court, which was serving as a makeshift dance floor. There was no live band. My father was an expert with electronics and sound systems. He received most new records free from producers. He had made what today would be called "mixes," tape cassettes with various songs on them. My friends and I ate food and danced to the taped music beneath the tent. For the time and place, it was meant to be very restrained and genteel.

But in one regard, there was no restraint at all: the presents. In that neighborhood, in those days, a bar mitzvah boy received a fortune in gifts. Cash and savings bonds. Gold watches and gold pen sets, not one but half a dozen of each, maybe more. Silver identity bracelets that were the current fad. Money clips and tie clips, chains and rings set with diamonds and other precious gems.

I've never worn much jewelry. I don't like the feel of it against my skin. For decades, I never wore even a wedding band or a wristwatch. So a lot of these baubles weren't actually useful to me. But I was absolutely dazzled by the worth of them. It was the first wealth that ever belonged entirely to me. Before that, I had once saved my allowance for months to put together forty dollars to buy a rare stamp. This, though, this was—who knows how much?—thousands and thousands of dollars' worth of precious metals, gems, and legal tender. Riches beyond my imagination, and it was all mine.

I collected the haul in an elegant leather box that was itself one of the gifts. I stored the box in a toy cabinet built into my bedroom wall. In the days and weeks that followed, I would take the box out of the cabinet sometimes. I would sit on my bed and hold the box on my legs and open the lid and gaze down at the contents. I would run my fingers over the chains and pens and watches. I would sort them in the box's various compartments and try to guess at their value. It seemed a sparkling treasure to me, like the contents of Aladdin's cave.

I don't know how long my enchantment lasted. Six months maybe, maybe eight, summer into spring. But slowly over that time, a deep misgiving grew in me. I would open my treasure box and find my delight in my wealth had become intermingled with a sense of self-reproach. There was something wrong with this, wasn't there? At first, I couldn't admit to myself what it was. But then I could, and my guilt soured to anger. I would sit on the bed and stare down at the open box on my legs. I would stare down at the gold and the silver and the gems and the bonds. I would run my fingers over them and hear them clink and rattle. And I would think, *Why did you do it? Why did you let them make you do it? Why did you say those things that you did not believe in front of everyone? Why did you sing those prayers you did not even understand?*

I didn't think this then but I think so now: if deep down I had not believed in God, it would not have troubled me as much as it did. If you had asked me the question at the time, I probably would have come out with some pseudo-sophisticated agnostic blather about the unknowability of the infinite. But I'd have been conning you—posing, parroting the adults. I believed, all right. It was in my nature to believe. I felt God there. Why else would I have been so distressed? If it had not mattered to me that I had lied in a temple, at an altar, with the Torah open under my hands—if it had not mattered, I mean, in some essential spiritual way—I think my guilt and shame would have been less intense. I think they would have faded away in time.

But they did not fade. As the months went on, they grew stronger. I grew angry at myself. I grew angry at my parents. I grew angry—not at Judaism specifically but at religion in general. I resented the whole machinery of godless ritual and mindless tradition. I resented its authority without integrity, big people wielding their power over small. With great pomp and sacred ceremony, they had made me declare what I did not believe was true—and then *they had paid me for the lie with these trinkets!* I felt that I had sold my soul.

Now, when I opened the leather box, when I looked down at the gold and silver and gems and US Bonds, it was a bitter, bitter thing. Even the pleasant chill of metal seemed to have faded from the stuff. It felt warm and clammy under my fingertips. I took the box out of its cabinet less and less often and finally not at all; I just left it in there. I pushed it to the back of its shelf, stacking old board games in front of it. Even so, even with the cabinet door shut, I felt its presence, a weight, a sorrow, an accusation.

Finally, one night, after I'd gone to bed, I forced myself to stay awake. I waited in the dark for more than an hour. My father had to go to work so early in the morning that he was often asleep by nine, by ten at the latest. By midnight, usually, the whole house was quiet. When I felt I'd waited long enough, I opened the toy cabinet—quietly, quietly. I slid the boxes of board games aside. I drew out the leather box full of jewels. Barefoot in my pajamas, I crept downstairs with the box tucked under my arm.

Just in back of the house, down a flight of three steps, there was a concrete platform. It was set beneath the kitchen window, beside the cellar door. Two garbage receptacles were built into the cement, side by side. When you wanted to open one, you would step on a foot pedal to lever up the iron lid. Then you could lower in the old grocery bags full of kitchen trash.

I remember—I can feel it as I write—the cold of the concrete on my bare feet as I hurried tiptoe down those steps. I can still feel the rough surface of the cement through the knees of my pajamas as I knelt on the platform beside the receptacle. I pressed on the foot pedal with one hand to lift the iron lid. I can still feel the cold of the iron against my palm. With the other hand, I stuffed the leather box into the sodden garbage bag. I remember—I can feel as I write—the damp coffee grounds and the brittle egg shells that rose around my forearm as I worked the box deep, deep into the trash. I wanted to make sure it would not be discovered before the garbage men came in the morning and took the bags away. When the leather treasure box was well hidden, I lowered the heavy lid carefully so it wouldn't make a noise.

I crept back inside—crept quickly back upstairs, two stairs by two. I slipped back into my bedroom, closing the door behind me.

CHAPTER 4

A CHRISTMAS CAROL

When did I first become aware of Jesus Christ? Every idea comes with its own history. What was the history of this idea in me? During those months of self-searching in the hills above Santa Barbara, I asked myself that question continually. I had heard a call to be baptized, but why? Why baptized? Why Christ?

The thing was, the figure of Jesus had been at the center of my thinking for a long time. Even before I had any faith at all, I had written an entire novel about him—two novels, in fact, though the second was just a slapdash abridgment of the first, as I'll explain. By the time the call to baptism came to me, I did have faith, a general faith in God. And yes, the God I believed in looked very much like the God of the New Testament: the *logos* of Love that redeemed a tragic world. But that only begged the question: Why? Why that God? Why Christ?

Finding the answer was not as simple for me as it would

have been for someone who had been raised in a Christian household. As a child, I had never been taught that Jesus was even special, let alone divine. I couldn't recall ever having been inside a church as a boy. I don't think I seriously discussed Jesus with any of my little Christian friends. I didn't *have* that many Christian friends, only a few. Mostly, I grew up a Jew among other Jews. So how had Jesus entered my imagination? How had he come to occupy its core?

It took an effort of memory, but after a while I reached back and recalled the first time I truly noticed him. It happened on a Christmas Eve. I don't know how young I was, but young, a little boy, five or six maybe. I had been sent to stay overnight at the house of a woman named Mina.

Mina had come to work for my family shortly after my younger brothers were born. My older brother was six then and I was three. With the two of us underfoot already, my mother needed help taking care of baby twins. Mina came to live with us for a while, a year or so, I don't know how long exactly. But even after she moved out, she remained our regular babysitter. She was more than that to me, though, much more. To me, she was almost a second mother.

My first mother—my real mother—was an enigmatic figure. I find, when I try to describe her, pale adjectives replace the living presence. Restrained. Self-protective. Gracious with strangers; they loved her. With her family . . . not cold, no. But aloof. Purposely insubstantial, somehow. Emotionally invisible. Even in my memories, the light seems to pass right through her, making her difficult to see. I can get at nothing solid about her but her fears and foibles and unfulfilled desires. She was afraid of authority figures. She yearned for a more glittery and urban life. She was afraid of testing herself and her talents. She was afraid to fail. I remember one or two titanic and terrifying rages from her, one or two shockingly icy and cruel remarks. But those were rare moments when she flashed into relief, a ghost revealed by lightning. Mostly, she was atmosphere.

Mina, on the other hand, was nothing if not a vivid personality. She only stood about five feet tall, if that, but they were five feet of gruff peasant cheer and practical energy. A Yugoslavian immigrant with a thick accent, she was lavishly affectionate, comically quaint, and down to earth. She never learned to speak good English and I sometimes had to help her read hard words. But she knew what she was about, all right.

I remember her making beds and cleaning rooms with curt, blunt, almost military efficiency. Chasing my brothers and me around here and there. Laughing, scolding, tickling, threatening to spank but never actually doing it. Driving us with elaborate care in her galumphing jalopy of a car. Always cooking something or baking something, sometimes both at once. I don't remember ever seeing her sit still to look at a book or magazine. Even when she'd watch TV with us, she'd get so involved in the story she would shout at the hero—"Look out!"—to warn him that the villain was sneaking up behind him. It used to drive us crazy. We tried again and again to explain to her that the characters on screen couldn't hear her. She'd just laugh at her own silliness and go right on.

She lived with her family in a tidy little clapboard house in the nearby town of Port Washington. It was a working-class enclave at the time, distinctly lower on the social and economic scale than Great Neck. Her family, as I understood it, was a collection of refugees, chased out of southeastern Europe by the Nazis or the Communists, I was never sure which. There was her older sister, the widow of a German Luftwaffe pilot who'd been shot down in the war. She was gaunt and tart and rather Germanic herself, but kindly for all that. Then there was their brother, a carpenter, who had come to America in time to serve in Korea. He'd been badly injured there when his jeep overturned. He'd had a metal plate installed in his head and was never quite right afterward. A sweet-natured, jolly enough fellow most of the time, he was given to sudden bouts of obsessive agitation, flashbacks to combat, and depressive drinking binges.

Finally there was Mina's niece, the daughter of her sister and the dead Luftwaffe guy. She was in her teens then, about ten years older than me. She used to babysit us sometimes. She was a gentle, dreamy girl of truly astounding beauty, blond and slender and delicate as a porcelain figurine. Her ethereal personality turned out to be the forewarning of a mental illness that blighted her adulthood—schizophrenia, I think. But back then, she was always just very kind and soft and patient with me, and I . . . ? I fell so deeply in love with her that she left a permanent impression on my soul. Her face became my standard of beauty. Her name became my favorite female name. Sweet, gentle, mentally ill women turn up with alarming regularity as characters in my novels. The psychiatrist's patient in *Don't Say a Word*, the mother in *Empire of Lies*, the hero's friend in the young adult story *Crazy Dangerous*. I'm sure there are more of them. They're all she. Conjuring her this very moment, I can feel again the pang of my childish devotion. I never got over her.

I'm not sure how much of Mina's family history I've gotten right here. I'm not sure how much of what I've gotten right is true. This is just what I knew about them, or thought I knew, when I was little. My parents used to hint that the sister and the Luftwaffe pilot had never really gotten married, that it was a wartime fling and the beautiful niece whom I loved was illegitimate. In later years, I myself sometimes wondered if the whole family wasn't actually German, if they hadn't pretended to be Yugoslavian to avoid the anger that Americans, and especially Jews, still felt toward Germans after the war.

Never mind, though. None of that bothered me when I was a child. None of it bothers me now. Mina and her family simply became part of my family. And Mina gave me a substantial portion of what mothering I had.

My own mother resented motherhood. "Even a cat can have kittens," she once told me bitterly. She loved her children, but she had no use for the day-to-day job of us. She didn't like to cook, for instance. I think Mina taught her every recipe she knew. I don't remember Mom ever going to a PTA meeting or volunteering to participate in a school event. She did show up for all the mom necessities. She nursed us through our illnesses. She dispelled our nightmares. She dried our tears and bandaged our bruises after our Western-movie-sized brawls. But she generally performed these tasks with a brusque air of impatience and distraction. She was not like other moms we knew who seemed to mother with their whole selves and as if by nature.

Mina, though, who had no husband or babies of her own, nurtured children as she nurtured everyone else around her. She just took care of people, that's all. She took care of her own family—she ended up supporting the lot of them as they declined into disability and old age. She took care of babies as an obstetrics aide at a local hospital. She was a nanny to other families as well as ours. She even won awards for the charity work and church work she did all around her town.

Much of what she was expressed itself in the kitchen, her dominion. She was an incredible country cook, and her baking was beyond the power of praise. For us children, of course, this was the best thing about her. The Weiner schnitzels she sometimes made us, the steaks, the enormous but nonetheless crispy french fries—incomparable delights of my childhood. And next to the taste of the pastries and cookies she created, all other physical sensations of pleasure paled! It was she who baked our birthday cakes every year. (It was considered bad luck if she spelled your name right in the icing, which thankfully she never did.) But her Christmas cookies, or Mina Cookies as we called them, these were her unbelievably delicious masterpieces.

The impression those cookies made on me was deep, very deep. When I was forty, I went to Germany for the first time, to Munich. It was right around Christmas. I stepped into the famous *Christkindl Markt* in Marienplatz: a huge seasonal market in the city's main square. I took one whiff of the baked goods on sale in the stalls and I was thunderstruck by a visceral, Proustian sense of having stepped into my own memories. It was the smell of Mina Cookies. It was the smell of home.

We did not celebrate Christmas at my house. Or that is, we did for a while, and then we didn't. It was never a big event, even when we celebrated it. Hanukkah with its nightly candle-lighting ceremony, its eight days of one present after another—that was really the main attraction. But when I was very little, my father's radio partner, Dee Finch, a churchgoing Protestant of some sort, would send over a few gifts. We would find them hidden behind a chair on Christmas morning.

Then, one afternoon, as I was playing in the dining room, I overheard my mother talking on the phone in the kitchen. She was speaking to Finch's wife. She was asking her not to send us Christmas presents anymore. It was "too much" for my brothers and me to have Christmas and Hanukkah both, she said. Looking back, I've come to feel that she was acting on a directive from my father. I think he was moving to protect our Jewish heritage from the seductions of the Christmas festivities all around us. In fact, I have a sweet memory, dating from about this time, of Dad trying to fill the role of Santa Claus in our lives with a character named Hanukkah Harry.[1] He played the right Jewish old elf himself, of course. I remember giggling uncontrollably as he took my brothers and me on his knee one after another and listened to our present requests while responding in one of his funny voices.

At that moment, though—the moment when I overheard my mother on the phone—I was in no way concerned with matters religious. I remember my reaction very clearly. I didn't care about the loss of Christmas at all. But the presents! The loss of the presents! That, madam, was an outrage! I felt as if I had stumbled on a misguided, not to say evil, parental plot, a conspiracy to cause us to receive fewer gifts. Fewer gifts, I tell you! And the Finches gave good gifts too! Electric football games and those jumbo dump trucks that actually dumped. Really nice stuff. This was no small catastrophe.

I thought it stank and I didn't mind saying so. I lodged an eloquent protest, stomping back and forth in front of my mother across the kitchen floor as I declaimed on the injustice of it all. Maybe it was to mollify me—or maybe it was just an excuse to get rid of an annoying child for an evening—but in any case my mother arranged for me to stay overnight at Mina's house that Christmas Eve.

I don't think it had ever occurred to me that Mina was a Christian. I don't think I would have had any very clear conception of what that actually meant. She was, though. She was a true Christian. Religious, I mean, even devout. She went to church on Sunday. She said her prayers at night. She believed in supernatural presences and events with the faith of a child. She did the sort of charitable work in her community that my parents never did in ours. I don't think she ever mentioned Jesus to me, but he was alive and real to her. He was—as I see now—the reason she was the way she was, the reason she did the things she did.

Christmas at Mina's was an elaborate occasion. The little clapboard house in Port Washington was transformed into what, to me, was a wonderland. There was a towering fir tree scraping the ceiling in one corner of the small front parlor. Mina's brother climbed a ladder to string the colored lights on the branches while I stood below, craning my neck to watch him. Then I got to help hang the ornaments. And when the lights went on, reflected in the shining red and silver glass of the decorations, my mouth opened in an *o*.

Under the parlor windows—the windows that looked out onto the winter streets—there was a long table with a white cloth on it. The cloth was sprinkled with Styrofoam bits like snow. In the midst of the snow, a miniature village of porcelain country houses had been set up. Each house was lit from within by a tiny bulb. Tiny people—the policeman, the businessman with his briefcase, the mom with her carriage—stood on the lawns and sidewalks and streets. A train track encircled the town with a small electric train clacketing round and round on it. You could even put a white pellet in the loco-motive's smokestack so it would send up white smoke and give a whistle: *whoo-whoo*.

To decorate the windows themselves, the real windows above the porcelain village, I was given a pack of paper sten-cils and an aerosol spray can of synthetic frost. I would spray each stencil with the frost and the white powdery shape of it would appear on the glass: Santa Claus or a star or a winged angel. I cannot properly describe how much this delighted me or how beautiful I thought these frost shapes were.

In the corner opposite the tree, there sat the television set, an old black-and-white one in a wooden cabinet. On top of the cabinet was a record player, a turntable with a spindle at the center of it. A stack of records was held in place at the top of the spindle, and as each album finished, a new one dropped into place and began to play. The songs were sung by the then-still-living singers of an already-passing age: Frank Sinatra, Bing Crosby, Andy Williams, Ella Fitzgerald. There were carols of strangely elevated loveliness, like "Silent Night," "Adeste Fideles," and "O Little Town of Bethlehem." And there were more contemporary numbers—"Sleigh Ride," "Silver Bells," "White Christmas"—that had a rollicking but wistful charm of their own.

It was Christmas, in other words; a typical American Christmas. And maybe you'll say I'm describing what needs no description, what every American child has seen and heard for himself, in the movies if not in his own life. But I had not seen or heard it, not anywhere. It was all new to me.

And then, of course, there was the cooking. There was the warm, succulent smell of the cooking. There were Mina and her sister expertly weaving around each other in the kitchen, bickering as they cooked. Which was another thing about Mina's family, by the way. They bickered constantly. They were always nattering at one another over something or nothing, on and on in their cartoonish Old World accents. *You've turned the stove too high now. You're mixing too much sugar in the batter. If you don't put the oven mittens back where they belong, I can't find them when I need them.* I don't know why, but I found this delightful—vital and loving.

The adults at my house were far more decorous. My parents never squabbled like that at all. There was a sense that hostility was too dangerous, too combustible, to be discharged in playful sparks like that. My mother used to say that if she and my father ever fought—really fought—he would leave her, assuming the marriage was over. My father admitted that this was true. He said that, whenever he saw a couple quarreling, he simply assumed they were going to divorce. Mom and Dad were not cool or controlled with each other—not at all. They were very affectionate. But there was nothing like the unchecked badinage I heard in the kitchen at Mina's house. The meaningless spats dissipating into cackling laughter. *Now look what you've done, you'll burn the whole house down.* To me, it sounded like the chuck and crackle of logs on a hearthfire.

I was given a role to play in all this too: batter to mix, Mina Cookies to lay out on the pan. The mystery of how she made those chocolate and vanilla spirals was revealed to me at last. I got to lick the beater and scrape the batter bowl clean with a spoon, which may have been the single greatest thing that had ever happened to me up to that time. And the beautiful niece, who had been out with friends all evening, came home and petted me and fussed over me and I loved her so. And another record dropped down on the turntable.

I have been re-creating that Christmas all my life. When we first moved in together, my wife was mystified by the way my normally lofty cultural tastes metamorphosed every December into the predilections of a working-class Yugoslavian immigrant.

"You want to listen to Andy Williams music? Really?"

"I like Andy Williams."

"Since when?"

"And how come we don't have those paper things that you spray and they make angel shapes on the window?"

"Stencils? You want to stencil frost angels on my windows?"

"Why not? I like them. They're nice."

This is not to say that I came to believe in Christmas. I didn't believe in it. The trip to Bethlehem, the virgin birth, the shepherds watching their flocks by night, the three kings, the child in the manger, the salvation of the world: nice stories, but I didn't buy into any of it. It was a point of pride with me, in fact, that I didn't. I liked to tease my wife that only a secular Jew like myself could really appreciate the holiday as it deserved. For us, I told her, it was all trees and cookies and colored lights without any of that tiresome religious stuff to worry about. We had no bad memories of childhood Christmases to haunt us. No flashbacks to that time when Dad got drunk and told Uncle Bob what he really thought of him. We came to the day with a clean Jewish slate. We opened our presents. We watched *It's a Wonderful Life* on TV. Then we forgot the whole thing until next year.

But when I came to struggle with the idea of being baptized, when I asked myself how Jesus had first entered my consciousness, it was Christmas I remembered, that first Christmas at Mina's house.

It happened at the end of the evening. The music was turned off. The lights on the tree went dark. Mina took me upstairs to what would be my bedroom—and that's where Jesus was. It was a small and gloomy room, I remember. The bed, framed in dark-stained wood, nearly filled it corner to corner. On the wall, above the headboard, to my right as I was lying down looking up at it, there was a framed picture of Christ. It was a cheap print of some sentimental painting. It showed a long-haired goy gazing soulfully into the middle distance, his coiffed honey-brown locks surrounded by a golden glow. As an adult, I've always disliked pictures like that. I've always disliked the effeminate piety of them. They have no weight, no tragedy. It's a cotton-candy god to me: sugar and fluff. In the moment, though, the picture frightened me. To my child's eyes, it seemed downright eerie. This Jesus whom people prayed to in their churches: he looked other-worldly, spectral, weird. What was he gazing at like that, off in the distance? And why was he glowing? It was spooky.

I don't know if I'd ever slept away from home alone before. I wasn't scared about it exactly, but I was a little nervous. I was afraid of being afraid. I knew I wouldn't want to call for Mina if I had bad dreams or got anxious in the watches of the night. I wouldn't want to go sniveling for help in a strange household, especially with the pretty niece around to hear me. So then, how horrible it would be to have to lie alone and wide awake in the alien room with creaks and shadows all around me, and that creepy Jesus hanging over my head.

Mina turned out the light and left me. I lay in the bed beneath the picture. I was afraid to look at it, but I couldn't help myself. Every time I forced my eyes shut, I would sense that eerie presence up above me on the wall. From time to time, I would feel compelled to sneak a peek at him—just to make sure he hadn't moved, to make sure he wasn't suddenly staring down at me with a malevolent grin. I began to be afraid that the fear of him would keep me up all night.

It didn't, though. The Christmas Eve doings had exhausted me. Each time I shut my eyes, they remained closed a little longer. A few more minutes and I was fast asleep. An instant later, so it seemed, the first gray light of Christmas Day was at the window. I had made it to the end of the darkness. I was very relieved.

I had awakened early, earlier than the grown-ups. Though I was eager to go downstairs and see the presents under the tree, I was not comfortable enough in the strange house to get out of bed and go by myself. Instead, I lay there waiting for the adults to stir. As I lay, my eyes returned to the picture on the wall, to Christ.

How strange. He was not frightening anymore. He wasn't eerie or spooky or creepy, not at all. The morning light had dramatically transformed him. He seemed wholly benevolent to me now. Kindly. Powerful. Protective. In fact, though his expression was oh-so-elevated and very, very serious indeed, I thought I now detected a touch of humor at the corners of his mouth, a secret mirth. It was as if we shared a private joke together. It was as if we were both amused by the childish mistake I had made last night. In the darkness, I had been afraid that he was evil. At dawn, I realized he had been my friend and guardian, watching over me all night long.

More than forty years later, as I drove through the Santa Barbara hills, as I questioned the motives of my conversion, I thought of this Christmas morning again and again. It kept playing in my mind with new variations, like a theme in a fugue. It was so easy to make a psychological backstory out of it. Sensitive child, hostile father, unknowable mother, kindly babysitter, happy Christmas, picture of Christ. Well, no wonder I wanted to be baptized. No wonder I wanted to make that glowing *goyische* face the mask of God. No wonder I wanted to reduce the incomprehensible will of all creation to a magic gentile framed on a fondly remembered wall. It was just a psychological glitch, as it turned out. A nostalgic yearning for a sweet moment from my youth. Understandable enough. But it was no good reason to betray my commitment to reality. No reason to betray my heritage. No reason to dilute my writerly dedication to the hard, cold truth.

On the other hand, every idea comes with its own history, but that doesn't make it false. The genesis of a belief is no disproof of it. The truth remains true no matter how or why we come to find it. If there is a higher, spiritual, supernatural world, it stands to reason that this everyday, material, natural world is only the language in which it speaks to us. So maybe my psychology was just Christ's way of reaching me, his doorway into my heart. Maybe Mina's loving-kindness was just an image of his. Maybe the beauty of Christmas was just a symbol for his. Maybe that picture on the wall was a story he was telling me: "I, who seem fearsome in the mind's darkness, will reveal myself to be your savior by the light of day."

In any case, Christmas was a pleasure to me ever after. I have fond memories of many Decembers. I never stayed overnight at Mina's again, but my family would troop over to her house for a Christmas dinner every year, and it was always wonderful.

When I was eight years old, I discovered Charles Dickens's *A Christmas Carol.* There was a cartoon version of it on TV, starring the popular nearsighted character Mr. Magoo as the miserly Ebenezer Scrooge. I loved the story so much I begged my mom to buy me the novel. I was so proud to have read such a grown-up book by myself—and so disappointed when I realized it was an abridgment for children! When I was a year or two older, I watched the film version, the British one from 1951. I loved the spooky atmosphere, the frightening phantoms. I even appreciated the magnificent acting of Alistair Sim. He played Scrooge as a human being who really seemed to believe his own narrow philosophy. I still watch the movie with my family every year.

As for the original, the 1843 Dickens novella, I've come to feel it's one of the greatest works of wisdom literature ever created, up there with Job and Ecclesiastes and the *Tao te Ching*. Jacob Marley's tormented ghost asks Scrooge the one question on which everything depends: "Man of the worldly mind, do you believe in me or not?" The immortal soul might just be an illusion thrown up by the deceived senses. But if it's truly there, all the rest follows naturally: the justified pangs of conscience; the reality of love; the unity of personality through past, present, and future; the miracle of redemption. "It's all right," as Scrooge cries out in his joyous reclamation. "It's all true, it all happened."

Christmas became an essential part of my love life too. The winter I was seventeen, my then-girlfriend and I rented a house together in Indiana where she went to college. I smuggled the pieces of a bicycle into the cellar where I secretly assembled them during the day while she was at work. I can still see the look of surprise and delight on her face when the finished machine appeared wrapped in ribbons under our tree.

When I was nineteen, another girlfriend invited me to join her enormous Irish Catholic family for Christmas dinner. I was working as a newsman at a small radio station in Berkeley, California. Like many Jews in round-the-clock occupations, I had volunteered for the Christmas shift so the Christian workers could stay home. It was a miserable way to spend the day. All alone in the studio. No news to report. The only sound bite I could get was from some guy who'd had himself baptized in the campus fountain at the university: "It was cold!" I replayed those three words in every newscast until my boss called me from home and told me to knock it off. But what I remember most is the blast of warmth and good cheer that greeted me when I finally stumbled into my girlfriend's house. The company, the tree, the music, the food. What a relief. What a pleasure.

Later, when I moved in with the girl who would become my wife, and later still, when I married her, we'd spend Christmas at her parents' house. They always made a huge occasion of it, the presents spilling from beneath the tree almost to the opposite wall. I would sit up late with my wife's father, a brilliant professor and author. We would drink whiskey together and talk books and ideas until we could no longer keep our eyes open.

But he was an atheist. So was his wife, my wife's mother. My wife was, too, for that matter. We all were atheists or agnostics, the lot of us. It was Christmas we loved, the bright tradition, not Christ, never Christ. The holiday had simply become my deracinated version of my father's Passover: a celebration emptied of its meaning.

In the end, as I considered my conversion, I thought: No. It wasn't that night at Mina's house that made Jesus Christ central to my thinking. It wasn't that picture on the wall that made his presence pervasive in my imagination. It wasn't even the Christmases through the following years that made him matter to me so much.

It was stories. It was literature. He came to me that way.

CHAPTER 5

TOUGH GUYS

I've always loved tales of adventure. Stories of suspense, action, danger, fear. Superheroes against arch-villains. Cops against killers. Men against monsters. As a boy, I couldn't get enough of monsters. Creatures limping through misty graveyards in the dead of night—they were some of my favorite things. When I was seven, the Aurora company started bringing out plastic monster models from the old Universal movies I loved to watch on TV. They were thirteen-inch-tall figurines that came in pieces that you assembled and glued together, painting them if you liked. Frankenstein, Dracula, the Wolfman, the Mummy, the Creature from the Black Lagoon, and so on. I got them all, every one. My mother worried I was growing morbid. When I was ten, I had to beg her to let me buy the new *Creepy* magazine. But oh man, I had to have it. A monthly collection of black-and-white comic strip spook stories with macabre twist endings. The vampire turned out to be the heroine's suitor. The werewolf turned out to be the hero's wife. The last line of dialogue was almost always the same wordless shriek of terror: "Aiiiyeeeeee!"

Alfred Hitchcock, though, he was my Homer. He was a movie director first, of course, but as the "master of suspense," he also became a brand. That was my brand. I never missed his weekly TV show, *Alfred Hitchcock Presents*. A new tale of murder and mayhem every week. More macabre twist endings. The killer wife feeds her husband's body to the police disguised as a leg of lamb. A wife identifies her rapist and her husband kills him, but the wife has gone mad and is pointing at every man she sees.

Sometimes when the show was on, my best friend and I would build a tent of blankets and chairs in my bedroom to create a spooky inner chamber. We'd roll the wheeled television stand under the canopy and sit on the floor cross-legged, gazing up at the screen. I read Hitchcock-brand short-story anthologies, too, and listened to the record *Alfred Hitchcock's Ghost Stories for Children* until I knew Saki's *Open Window* almost by heart. And of course I subscribed to the monthly *Alfred Hitchcock Mystery Magazine*. When I was in my early thirties, one of my first suspense stories was published there. It touched me deeply to see my own sentences on those much-beloved, pulpy pages.

As for Hitchcock's movies, they were my favorites, not just of all movies but of all stories anywhere. Innocent men drawn into spy chases and murder plots. Glamorous women caught in traps of suspicion and fear. The weird, sexy tension of *Rear*

Window and *Vertigo* had a special power over me. A house-bound man thinks he might have witnessed a murder in the apartment across the way. A broken cop falls in love with a woman who may be possessed by the dead.

Each film was aired on television only once or twice when I was a boy.[1] Then, tangled in legal complications, the movies were not shown for more than twenty years. As a result, they became locked away in my unconscious. They worked on my brain in there, shaping it unseen. When the films were finally re-released, just as I was turning thirty, one of my brothers and I went to the theater to see them. I was stunned to discover how much of my sense of plotting and timing they had formed without my knowing it. "That Alfred Hitchcock," I remarked to my brother when the show was over, "he stole everything from me!"

In my teens, I discovered the tough-guy writers. My older brother introduced me to the existential adventure tales of Ernest Hemingway, his favorite. I discovered the hardboiled detective stories of Dashiell Hammett and Raymond Chandler on my own.

Toughness was always an ethos in my house. I don't mean physical toughness necessarily, though that played a part. I'm talking about an attitude of mind: being tough, being cynical, unsentimental, sardonic, detached. That was the way a man was, a real man, or so we believed. A real man didn't get taken in by sloppy romantic ideals like Honor or Sacrifice or Faith or Charity. He didn't fall into line behind whatever hypocrite was mouthing rah-rah moral platitudes for the crowd.

Group loyalty was for fools. School spirit? Patriotism? They were sucker games. If we identified as Jews, it was because we wouldn't be pushed around by gentiles, not because we cared all that much about other Jews. If we stood by our family, it was because we knew no one else could be counted on. But we also knew that our family—that all families—were snakepits of envy and hostility. In the end, let's face it, pal, you lived and died alone.

This attitude originated with my father. It was his personality translated into a worldview.

For twenty-five years, my father was one of the most popular radio entertainers on the air. He was never a national star, but his top-rated show was on during "morning drive," the most important time slot, in New York City, the biggest market there was. Even aside from his talent and success, there was much to admire about the man. He was honest in business. He had integrity in his art. He was decent and fair to the people who worked with him. Most importantly from my perspective, he was always kind and loving and respectful toward my mother.

But he was a comedian, and not just by profession but by nature too. And like every comedian I've ever met, he was angry at his core. His sharp, biting, antic wit bubbled up from an inner cauldron of seething rage. The world was unfair, a conspiracy of big guys against the little guy, namely him. His comedy was a camouflaged hand grenade. *Just kidding: kaboom!* Intellectual sabotage against the machinery of life.

He had a chip on his shoulder, in other words. A whole

stack of chips. About being a Jew in a Gentile universe, about the fact he never finished college, about the fact that serious people never took his ideas seriously. Most of all, he was deeply bitter that he never achieved the wide-ranging fame of other Jewish comics like Danny Kaye and Jerry Lewis.

But then, he never had the broad appeal of stars like them. They were sleek, handsome, charming, upbeat, and essentially sentimental. My dad was fat, bald, bespectacled, and barbed. He was not made for the nation as a whole. He was a New Yorker through and through. He loved the frenetic individualism of the city. He loved its million minds and dialects, almost all of which he could imitate to perfection. He loved the chaos, most especially. He didn't even like to see New Yorkers politely standing in line for a bus. Too orderly, he said, too organized, the first small sign of fascism on the march. For a Jew, the city's chaos was safety. Out there—out in the bland, farmer-faced homogeneity of the fruited plains beyond the Hudson—a Jew stood out like a sore thumb and was always in peril. Here, in Bigtown, he could get lost on the pushing, shoving, arguing, watch-where-you're-going-buster streets. If life on those streets sometimes seemed like a Hobbesian war of all against all, it was still better than a Hitlerian war of all against him!

My father had a story he liked to tell about his own father. Grandpa was a Lithuanian immigrant. A tough, domineering, sometimes violent man. He ultimately became a pawnbroker in a run-down, black neighborhood of Baltimore. But before that, for a time he lived in a small town—in Maryland somewhere or upstate New York, I don't remember. In any case, one night a fire erupted in the town. The flames raged through the buildings of Main Street, leaping store to store. Then they spread to the private houses beyond. As the disaster became unstoppable, the town leaders hurriedly called an emergency meeting—and elected my grandfather fire chief because he was the only Jew around to take the blame!

That story is too good to believe and too funny to check, but it gives you a sense of my dad's perspective. It was a perspective imbued with fear—fear of the Man, of the State, of the Power, fear of the *goyische* streets of Anytown where every gentile was a Cossack Waiting to Happen, if not a Nazi in Disguise. Dad joked about that fear a lot. *Don't make trouble; they'll come and take you away!* But the fear was real, and it kept his mind buzzing like an electric spark between the two poles of anxiety and rage.

People were not to be trusted. They were envious, hostile—all of them. This is another trait I've seen in many comedians. They all seem to feel that someone's cheated them out of something. My father likewise. He knew the secret reason why everyone was out to thwart him. If he couldn't sell a screenplay he'd written, it was because the producer was jealous of people who were multitalented. If an editor wouldn't publish his book, it was because he was too stuck-up to believe a mere funnyman might have something interesting to say. And, of course, like every artist who's ever been rejected, Dad knew the hidden truth about every publisher and movie studio and television producer alive: *It's just about money to them. All they want is to sell mediocre garbage to the lowest common denominator!* But you couldn't say that too loudly, or they would come and take you away.

Even if someone hadn't committed a transgression against him personally, Dad could still always spot a member of a transgressive class. Intrusive executives. Fascist Republicans. Stormtrooper cops. Intellectuals were especially suspect. College professors: pretentious snobs, the lot of them; thought they were better than you were. Teachers in general: they were just people who couldn't make it in the "real world." Those who can, do; those who can't, teach. If an English teacher so much as criticized one of his sons' papers, Dad would say it was only because he or she was a frustrated writer, jealous of our talent.

No one simply had an opinion in Dad's world. No one was trying to do his best with the best of wills. Everyone had an angle, or a personal failing—fear, greed, guilt—that caused him to work against you, to get in the way of your success. And, of course, anyone who belonged to any group of any kind that hadn't come to the aid of the Jews during the Holocaust— Germans, Frenchmen, Poles, gentiles—oh, why mince words, everyone, including the Jews themselves!—was obviously not going to be on your side when the danger waters rose.

Some part of this attitude, I think, was the expression of a ferociously competitive man in an insanely competitive business. I don't know how it is today, but back then, the average length of a New York DJ's career was about as long as a finger-snap. They came and went, fanfare followed hard by taps. The radio guys I met were all terrified of being fired. I remember one of Dad's colleagues at the station where he worked—call him Bob, not his real name. Bob would call the house almost daily to ask if his job was in danger. Finally, my father stopped taking his calls and told us kids to tell Bob he wasn't at home. I remember I answered the phone once, and it was Bob.

Hey, spunky, it's Bob! Is your dad there?

He's not home.

Listen, I just have to ask him one thing.

He's not home, Bob.

Really?

Yeah.

You sure?

Yeah, positive. He's not home.

Okay. Well, listen . . . have you *heard anything about me getting fired?*

Bob, I'm ten years old!

Tough business, show business. You couldn't blame the old man for being on watch. Everyone was a rival. Those who were beneath you were looking for their chance to climb over you. Those who were above you couldn't possibly deserve it and so had clearly cheated you. My dad never even praised his sons without disparaging the competition. I was never just good in the school play; I was always better than everybody else. That's why I didn't get the starring role. They were all envious of me. Tough business, those school plays. Everyone out for himself.

My father was not just the head of our household, he was its center. A big, vociferous personality, he had a show-biz narcissist's gift for drawing others into his mental scenarios.

We were all partisans in his war against the Great Thwart-You Machine. His hostile and paranoid mind-set surrounded us like mist. We breathed it in. We saw the landscape through it. It became the hue of our environment.

For me, though, my father's inner world was not a pleasant place to be. From early on, I did not want to live there. He knew it, and it made him mad.

There were four of us, four boys. The eldest was three years older than me. The youngest, fraternal twins, were three years younger. Toward me, the middle child, my father conceived a special animosity.

Maybe it was because I was stubborn in my opinions. Maybe it was because I was a dreamer off in a world of my own. I don't know. There was just something about me he could not abide. From my youngest years, he hit me, ridiculed me, and browbeat me in a way he did not my brothers. My older brother once told me that Dad was so unkind to me it actually frightened *him*. As a result, though I admired his scrappy integrity as a man, and though I would one day emulate his loving-kindness as a husband, I neither liked nor trusted him as a father—never did, never came to.

When I was in my twenties, my father told me I had always seemed to him a "stern presence." I suppose he felt I judged him harshly. I suppose I did. I remember thinking as a very young person, maybe only eleven or twelve: *This man is not on my side. He is not out to help me but to hurt me.* I consciously set out to develop a coldness at my deep center to protect myself from his sarcasm and abuse. I consciously set a perimeter around my point of view. I did not think the world was what he said it was and I would not change my mind to suit him, no matter how he screamed at me or laughed at me. My independence only inflamed his hostility toward me even more. Through my teens and even into my late twenties, our relationship was one long, furious firefight. He wanted me to see the world as he saw it. I refused. He wanted my piece of protected inner territory for his own. I would not give it to him.

That said, like any son, I grew up within my father's value system. It was the house I lived in. Even when we were at odds, it was often impossible for me to tell what was my own independent opinion and what was a rebellion against his. His worldview was part of me, so even when I struggled against it, I was engaged in a painful struggle against myself. It became harder and harder for me to know which was which, and who I really was.

To try to find the answer, I looked for other role models, other men I wanted to be like. That was why the tough guys caught my imagination the way they did. Hemingway, Hammett, and Chandler in books. Humphrey Bogart and John Wayne in the old movies on TV. The characters they wrote about and portrayed were fictional men I could model myself after when real men failed me.

Ironically enough, there were many ways in which these writers and movie stars simply served to Americanize my father's Old World values. In tough-guy movies and tough-guy books, Dad's hostile and hilarious Jewish antagonism toward the powers-that-be was recast into the tight-lipped solitude of the incorruptible American hero. Dad's fearful-angry, hit-and-hide joke-jabs at authority became Rick Blaine's small, hidden acts of defiance in *Casablanca*. *I stick my neck out for nobody.* My dad's working-class anti-intellectualism became Jake Barnes's war-weary existentialism: *I did not care what it was all about. All I wanted to know was how to live in it* from Hemingway's *The Sun Also Rises*. My father's Ashkenazi suspicion of group loyalty and high sentiment became Frederic Henry's heroic desertion from the field of battle in *A Farewell to Arms*: *The things that were glorious had no glory.*

My father was waging a guerrilla war of comedy against the all-powerful Ministry of Earth—because he was a Jew, because he was an up-and-comer with a dozen chips on his shoulder, because he was an ambitious showman who wanted more recognition than he had, because he was the second son of a gruff immigrant tyrant who once punched a man so hard the guy actually rolled out of his pawnshop—because of whatever, whatever makes any of us what we are.

But the tough guys—the Bogart characters, the Hemingway characters, Hammett's detective Sam Spade—they stood apart from the mainstream for another reason, a better reason, or at least a reason that seemed more attractive to a young American boy. They stood apart because they had seen the Old World come falling down. The Great War, World War I, had brought an end to the high culture of Europe. The tough guys had seen that culture and its values in ruins. They had set out to form new values, their own values, values by which a modern man might live in a land gone bad.

It may seem silly—it may actually *be* silly!—that a 1960s teenager ensconced in one of the most comfortable suburbs in America searched for his male role models among fictional expatriates, world warriors, and private eyes from the 1920s, '30s, and '40s. But it did make a kind of sense. Not only did these characters rework my father's neurotic antagonism toward his environment into something admirable and manly; they were also dealing with issues that were the issues of my day.

Because my culture, too, the culture of my childhood, was falling, was fallen. The collapse was unfolding on our television screens, in the background of my life. There were murders of high-profile public figures. Martin Luther King Jr. Senator Robert Kennedy—whom I had seen in person when he spoke at a local shopping mall what must have been mere months before his death. There were riots and protests against the way things were. Against racism in the South. Against the war in Vietnam. Against the very capitalism and churchgoing morality that made America what it had been at its height.

These events seemed far away from the immediate concerns of a self-absorbed fourteen-year-old, but they changed the atmosphere around me. They changed everything. We had grown up playing at being brave American GIs in our backyards. Now college students only a few years older than us were burning the American flag, praising our Communist enemies, and spitting on GIs in airports as they returned home from the battlefield. As children, we had wondered if we would have the courage to fight in a war as our fathers had.

Now these kids were dodging the draft and parading themselves as heroes for doing it.

But then, all the rules were shattering like glass. A year before, at thirteen, I would have said—all my friends would have said—that sex was only for married people. A young man might have a premarital fling or two with a bad girl, a loose girl, but when the time came to settle down, you married a nice girl, a virgin. A year later, when I was fifteen, I was having sex with girls who had seemed to me perfectly nice the year before and indeed seemed perfectly nice still, even naked in the park and in my bed. When my father found out what I was up to, he called one of my girlfriends "a whore." I was not just hurt, I was startled. He didn't understand: everything had changed. Nice girls did this now. It was what was happening.

There were drugs suddenly too. Marijuana, LSD, pills of various sorts, and occasionally cocaine. I smoked pot a few times, but I didn't like it. I never touched the harder stuff. It frightened me. I already knew I wanted to be a writer, and I was worried drugs would destroy my instrument, my brain. Anyway, toking weed, popping pills, snorting powder—it all seemed a bit effeminate to me. My heroes drank. Bogart, Jake Barnes, Philip Marlowe—they all hit the booze. I started doing that at fifteen too. I was soon hiding a pint of scotch outside a ground-floor window. I would leave the house by the front door, scoot around to the side, and retrieve the whiskey, then head off to join my friends.

The world I had grown up in was spinning away. Through a special program for troublesome kids, I graduated from high school a year early, but later, when a pal brought around a copy of the yearbook for my class, I was shocked by what I saw. All those graduation photographs of scrubbed, brightly smiling teenaged faces, all those nice, mostly Jewish boys and girls I had known. I thought they'd all be college-bound now, profession-bound, marriage and family bound, clean and perfect. But no. Not all. My pal pointed to picture after picture: This girl had gotten pregnant and had had an abortion; this girl had left school to have her baby in secret; this boy had run away from home to California; this boy and this boy had been arrested for drug use. There were overdoses. There was a suicide and a suicide attempt. There was even one boy, one of my best friends in elementary school, who had taken LSD while in the city one day and then stepped in front of a subway train.

In the ruined world after the Great War, the tough-guy writers had tried to build new moral codes of their own. In my peaceful and comfortable suburb, I tried to do the same. I tried each tough-guy's system on for size. I tried Jake Barnes's existentialism. I tried Sam Spade's nihilism. I even tried Rick Blaine's watchful detachment. I imitated these characters and tried to bring my habits of mind into line with theirs.

But each code seemed somehow insufficient to my purposes. Just as I wanted my daydreams to make sense as stories, I wanted my personal philosophy to make sense too. And I couldn't help noticing that at the core of many tough-guy fictions, there was actually something that was not so tough.

For instance, I love the movie *Casablanca*. Who doesn't? No matter how many egghead critics declare *Citizen Kane* to be the greatest American movie, we all know it's *Casablanca* in fact. A brokenhearted nightclub owner stands aside from the great struggle of World War II, but when his old lover returns to him, he finds, in moral sacrifice, his better self. The story is so grand and romantic, it makes real life seem too small. But I remember, when I was in my teens, it occurred to me that the uplifting end of the film redeems a main character who has really not behaved very admirably through the rest. If you strip Rick Blaine of Humphrey Bogart's wry, cool persona—if you take away the background music and the wonderful dialogue and the exotic locale—you're left with a guy who's kind of a crybaby for most of the picture. *You're not going to fight World War II because your girlfriend dumped you? Really? I mean, dude, it's World War II! Boo-hoo and all that, but get some perspective! Act like a man!*

Likewise, it came to seem to me that the romance of Hemingway's alcoholic drifters in *The Sun Also Rises* was essentially a romance of weakness and brokenness. *The war has left the world in ruins. We drink. We fish. We wander about. We complain a lot. Then we're done.*

As for Sam Spade in *The Maltese Falcon*, well, he was different. He was genuinely hardboiled. He sent the woman he loved to the gallows just because. That's hardboiled, for sure. But really, what sort of reason was that, when you came down to it? It wasn't as if he stood for justice. He stood for nothing. He believed in nothing. He did what he did because he was who he was and it was good for business. Again, when you took away the romance of the story and the glamour of the character, it was essentially the philosophy of a small-town shopkeeper. *I do what I do because I am what I am. I do what's good for business.*

One by one, the tough guys disappointed me as my father had disappointed me.

But then—then I read Raymond Chandler's *The Big Sleep*, and I discovered Philip Marlowe.

If there is one paragraph in all of fiction that transformed my life more than any other, it's the second paragraph of *The Big Sleep*. Professionally, it made me want to become a crime writer. Personally, it gave me an ideal of manhood that sticks with me still.

As the story begins, tough guy Los Angeles private eye Philip Marlowe has been summoned to the stately mansion of the elderly reprobate General Sternwood. Marlowe describes what he sees as he steps through the mansion's front door:

> The main hallway of the Sternwood place was two stories high. Over the entrance doors, which would have let in a troop of Indian elephants, there was a broad stained-glass panel showing a knight in dark armor rescuing a lady who was tied to a tree and didn't have any clothes on but some very long and convenient hair. The knight had pushed the vizor of his helmet back to be sociable, and he was fiddling with the knots on the ropes that tied the lady to the tree and not getting anywhere. I stood there and thought that if I lived in the house, I would sooner or later have to climb up there and help him. He didn't seem to be really trying.[2]

I remember I felt something swell inside me when I read this. I don't know why I grasped the idea of it so quickly. Maybe it was because it spoke into my old daydreams of rescuing girls from danger, I'm not sure. But for whatever reason, I understood the idea at once.

The knight of chivalric legend had never been real. Don Quixote had tried to emulate him and gone mad because life was not that way. But here, in the present day, even the *ideal* of the knight, the chivalric image of him, had been frozen into impotence on a stained-glass window, a window like a church's but in a sinner's mansion now. And here came a new fiction—a creation of the new city, a man of the modern world, a private eye—who carried that old ideal inside him, who would bring the hero on the stained glass back to life, not in irony like Quixote but in tragic earnest. Marlowe was a new American man determined to carry the old European ideal into the moral wasteland of the urban West.

"Down these mean streets a man must go who is not himself mean," Chandler famously wrote of his central character. "He is the hero; he is everything. He must be a complete man and a common man and yet an unusual man. He must be, to use a rather weathered phrase, a man of honor—by instinct, by inevitability, without thought of it, and certainly without saying it. He must be the best man in his world and a good enough man for any world."[3]

A man of honor in a world of corruption. Now that was a tough guy.

I read all of Chandler's Marlowe novels, all his short

stories, even a collection of his letters. I loved his writing like no writing I'd ever encountered before. I had my role model now. I wanted to be like Marlowe. I wanted to tell stories like Chandler's.

I wish I could report that this transformed me into a better person. More knightly, more noble, more chaste. Not at all. I was a teenager. I was angry. Foolish. And increasingly, I was twisted inside. What I imitated most in Marlowe was his heavy drinking.

But reading Chandler did have some good effects on me over the long run. For instance, I came upon this piece of advice in his letters: "The important thing is that there should be a space of time, say four hours a day at least when a professional writer doesn't do anything else but write. He doesn't have to write . . . But he is not to do any other positive thing . . ."[4] I began to follow that advice. I wrote my first full novel when I was fourteen. And yes, as a novel, it was every bit as excellent as you would imagine, but as a first exercise in self-discipline, it wasn't bad at all. That discipline became a habit and the habit solidified. It made me a productive writer even in the worst of times. It created a little space of sanity in days of deepening madness. I've written at least four steady hours, and usually more, every day for most of my life, and I think it saved my life at times.

There was also this. The image of a man carrying the ideals of a civilization within him, even when those ideals have crumbled around him, stuck with me through those chaotic years. I wanted to know more about those ideals. I wanted to learn where they came from. I wanted to hear the underlying reasons for them before joining my generation in deconstructing them and throwing them away.

So, after reading through the Marlowe novels, I turned to the old stories of knighthood. I started reading the Arthurian legends. Thomas Mallory and Chretien De Troyes, the Gawain poet, Tennyson, the *Once and Future King*. I always loved tales of adventure, and what could be more adventurous than the wars and duels, romances and adulteries of Camelot? Even as I continued to neglect my work at school, at home I studied the knights of the Round Table.

These stories were dense with Christian imagery. Of course they were. The church had virtually invented the code of chivalry as a way to convince real medieval knights to stop being the violent louts they were. In fiction, knights were courageous warriors for Christ, and ladies were virtuous in the Holy Virgin's name. The climactic Arthurian adventure—the quest for the Holy Grail—in most versions of the story was a search for the chalice from which Jesus poured wine at the Last Supper.

As it turned out, too, the symbols from these legends were strewn throughout all my favorite books. In Chandler's original Marlowe story, the knightly detective was actually named Mallory. *The Maltese Falcon*'s link to the Crusades gave the story overtones of the quest for the Holy Grail. The Grail mythology virtually dictated the plot of *The Sun Also Rises*—and that, in turn, connected the novel to T. S. Eliot's magnificent poem *The Wasteland*. Here was another writer— Eliot—who had seen the great culture of the West collapse and had tried to reconstruct its values within himself. I could see now why the poet had ultimately become a Christian.

In fact, by the time I was fifteen or so, I had begun to understand that Christianity was central to everything I had been reading. It was Christian ideas that had powered European culture, and it was belief in those ideas that had fallen when Europe's culture fell. The empty church in which Jake Barnes couldn't pray, the Holy Grail that Sam Spade found to be worthless, the stained-glass window that held Chandler's knight helpless, and the fragments of literature that Eliot shored against his ruins: these were the sad remnants of a founding faith that had all but gone out of the intellectual world.

I was only a boy still and I didn't understand much, but I began to understand that at the heart of all Western mythology, all Western civilization, all Western writing, all Western thought, and every Western ideal, there stood a single book, the Bible, and a single man, Jesus of Nazareth.

I decided I ought to find out more about them both.

CHAPTER 6

READING THE BIBLE

I had no religious motives in reading the New Testament. I wanted to be a writer. Christian symbolism was everywhere in the writing I admired. I wanted to know where the symbols came from. That really was all.

Of course, my family did not own a Bible with the New Testament in it. I had to go to the store and buy one. I don't remember where I got it, but the copy I bought is on the desk beside me as I write. A forty-five-year-old volume now, its binding is worn to the glue, its brown cover cracked and broken. Poignantly, I noticed only recently that it was published by Thomas Nelson, the same company that contracted me to write this book.

I decided to start with *The Gospel According to Saint Luke*. I think this was because I liked Christmas and Luke includes the Christmas story, which I had never read in the original. My older brother had recently left for college and I had inherited his coveted bedroom, down on the ground floor away from my parents' and younger brothers' rooms upstairs, so that's where I was when I started. It was a weekday evening, around dinner time. I closed my door, lay down on my bed, cracked open the book, and began to read.

Now, my father was a saboteur. He could not switch off his ferociously competitive instincts even when it came to his own sons. I believe it unnerved him to see us succeed at anything. I believe he was relieved to see us fail. I believe this was especially true when we aspired to accomplish something he hadn't or felt he couldn't accomplish himself. Whenever that happened, it always seemed to me he made extra efforts to thwart our ambitions by subtle and devious means.

I don't know whether he intended to do this. I don't even know if he knew he was doing it. It's possible he only sabotaged our projects in the same ways he often sabotaged his own. But speaking for myself, I found whenever he gave me professional advice, it was misguided. Whenever he introduced me to professional contacts, they turned out to be hapless or dishonest. Whenever he offered me financial assistance, it always came with a catch—some favor or side project I had to do in return that would somehow result in the ruination of my main purpose. From a very early age, I understood that if I wanted to succeed at anything in life, I would have to avoid my father's "help" at all costs.

This was certainly true when it came to my ambition to write novels. I had decided I would become a fiction writer on my fourteenth birthday. This was a Saturday in July. I was working a summer job as a busboy in a railroad station diner. It was a horrible job. Eight hours a day scraping half-eaten food off plates in a broiling basement kitchen. I was forbidden to talk to customers. I wasn't permitted to receive tips. I was constantly browbeaten by my bullying boss, an embittered Holocaust survivor who hated everyone, including me. Nonetheless, it was my first full-time job and I was proud of it. I had gotten it myself, starting at one end of the town's main drag and walking about three miles to the other end, stopping in every store along the way to ask for work. The diner was the last place I planned to try. They hired me on the spot.

I worked there two miserable weeks. Then, on my birthday, the owner suddenly "discovered" I was too young to be employed for such hours. I don't think I had lied to him about this. I suspect he had gotten into some sort of trouble over it or simply wanted an excuse to get rid of me. In any case, he called the house and spoke with my father. I was still asleep in bed when Dad burst into the room brimming over with glee and cried out with gusto, "Happy birthday! You're fired!"

I can't say I was heartbroken. It really was an awful place to work. But I didn't want to spend my summer idle either. I had started writing some adventure stories on an old portable typewriter. It was mostly kid's stuff I liked to share with my buddies at school. But now I decided I would try to go professional. I resolved to spend the summer writing stories and mailing them out to magazines. I followed the guidelines I had found in a helpful volume called *Writer's Market*. I would write my story, locate an appropriate magazine in the book, then mail my work to the editor with the required SASE—a Self-Addressed Stamped Envelope. Without fail, the magazine would promptly use the SASE to send the story back to me with a rejection slip attached. *Thank you for your submission. Unfortunately, your story does not fit our needs at this time.* Undaunted, I continued writing through that summer, then into the fall and winter and stubbornly through the years. I sold my first story five years later, when I was nineteen.

It's hard to remember now, but in those days, novelists were important cultural figures, the kings of narrative art. Celebrity writers like Norman Mailer and Gore Vidal were striving to fill the shoes of the idols of only one generation back, men so famous they went by a single name—Hemingway, Faulkner, Fitzgerald—as pop singers do today. Mine was a lofty ambition, in other words. And it was one my father shared. He wanted to write novels, too, and may have even tried it a couple of times, I don't know. I think the idea that I might succeed where he had not appalled him. In any case, almost from the moment I started writing seriously, my father began a nearly full-time campaign to derail my efforts.

It seems sadly hilarious to me now but at the time it was annoying and threatening. He would bombard me with absolutely terrible advice. *You can't work too many hours as a writer; you'll burn out. You can't have a job and write in your spare time—if you take a job, that's all you'll ever do. If you're not actually writing, you'll never be a writer—thinking and imagining are pretentious wastes of time. You have to write trash if you want to succeed.* The barrage of paternal words of wisdom that were not just untrue but the opposite of true was relentless.

Also, when I first started, he would occasionally convince me to show my work to someone he knew, usually someone with some tenuous connection to publishing. Inevitably, they would add their own bad and discouraging advice to his. *Try to write down to the audience more. You might consider going to law school so you have a backup plan.* One of them even told me that the market for pornography was quite strong so that might be a good place to start! After a few of these experiences, I began to refuse my father's offers of help, which left him hurt and furious.

What I remember most, though, are his interruptions. They were constant. Whenever my father heard my typewriter clacking, he would rush to the scene like a fireman to a fire. He would burst through the door without knocking and busy himself in my room with some meaningless chore sure to disturb the flow of my work. If I politely asked him to leave and let me get back to writing, he would become angry and verbally abusive, hurling four-letter curses at me. Once—so help me this is true!—he came in immediately after I started typing and began to lean over my shoulder to fiddle with the desk lamp directly above my page. "I just wanted to make sure this bulb didn't need changing," he said. Whatever pretense he used to enter, he would stay in my room until he felt he had broken my concentration. Only then would he withdraw.

This went on well into my adulthood. Taking the advice I had gotten from Raymond Chandler's letter, I would never do anything but write during my writing time. Most especially, I learned never to answer the phone. This drove my father crazy. He would call and let the phone ring twenty or thirty times until I unplugged it—maybe even after I unplugged it, for all I know. If my girlfriend picked up and told him I couldn't be disturbed, he would argue with her bitterly. Then he would call me later and berate me with foul-mouthed insults. After the answering machine was invented, he would snarl the four-letter words into the recorder and then loudly slam down the phone.

By then, though, I was out of his reach and power. In those earlier days when I was still living at home, I had to learn to take more elaborate countermeasures. I tried to arrange my work time for when he was out of the house. I worked in the basement with the washing machine rumbling to hide the rattle of my typewriter. Finally, I learned to write with a pen in a notebook—silently—and type the manuscript only after I was done with its composition. I continued to do that, in fact, until the personal computer came along a decade or so later.

As a result, even my silences became threatening to the old man. He started staging surprise raids on my room even when it was quiet.

So it was on that evening I lay down on my bed and began to read the New Testament for the first time. Rather than call me to dinner from afar as he always did with my brothers, my father made his way to my room and threw open the closed door without knocking to announce that dinnertime had come.

And what, to his absolute shock and horror, should he

discover but his own son lying there on the bed reading . . . *The Gospel According to Saint Luke!*

Oh, he was furious. *Furious.* The rage burbled out of him slow and thick like tar from a pit. He saw at once it was the Bible I was reading, and not the tremendous Old Testament he kept on a shelf in the den either, but something suspiciously compact and functional, the sort of thing some devious Christian might leave in a hotel room as an evangelical snare for unsuspecting alcoholics, homosexuals, and Jews!

When I set the book open, facedown on the desk so I could find my place again after dinner, he immediately snatched it up to examine it. Worse and worse! There, practically leaping off the page at him, were the words of Jesus Christ himself *piously highlighted in red.*

My friends at Thomas Nelson are lucky the old man's not alive today or he might hunt them down one by one. As for me, he let me know just what he thought of my reading material in no uncertain and no printable terms. It began slowly, with what I think were meant to be a few dismissive obscenities. But he clearly couldn't stop what was boiling up out of him. Soon, in a voice all the more unnerving for being murmurous and choked rather than explosively loud, he was coughing out a relentless stream of curses against both me and the fantastical sourcebook of our people's enemies.

I was actually taken aback. Like any teenager, I was perfectly capable of goading and provoking my parents. I'm sure I did many things purposely designed to defy, shock, and annoy them. But in this case, I was completely innocent. I had come to believe the Bible was central to Western literature. I wanted to work in the field of Western literature. So I was reading it. I wasn't brandishing the deadly volume at anyone. I was hidden away in my own bedroom behind a closed door. I didn't have the slightest thought of believing in the thing either. I just wanted to know what was in it.

I tried to explain some of this to my father as I followed him down the hall from my bedroom to the dining room. His anger was becoming frightening, all the more so for the low, strangled tone and the frozen smile with which he kept spitting out these obviously unstoppable obscenities. My explanation only galled him more. It stank of the intellectualism and cultural ambition that were part of what offended him about my writing in the first place.

Finally, as we reached the table where the rest of the family was waiting for us, he swiveled to me and pointed his finger in my face about half an inch from my nose. He said, "I hope you know that if you ever convert to Christianity, I'll disown you!" With that, he plonked himself down at the dinner table and ate without speaking another word.

Today, this memory makes me laugh. The idea of a father bursting in on his teenaged son and recoiling in horror to find him reading—the Bible! When you think what he easily *could* have found me reading—what he could have actually caught me *doing* in those wild days! The incident almost seems like a sketch from a television comedy show.

But I do want to be fair to the old man. He's no longer here to defend himself, for one thing. And for another thing, he was often so kind to so many people who did not happen to be me, he does not deserve to be remembered solely for the wrath I inspired in him. There was just something about me that made him mad, that's all. We were a bad father-and-son combination. It happens.

The full truth is, he had other good reasons to be concerned about my religious loyalties. The previous December, we had had one of the opening battles of what would become our ongoing war of wills. The cause had been nothing less than my refusal to celebrate Hanukkah with the rest of the family.

My bar mitzvah had been a slow-motion trauma for me. I never wanted to go through anything like it again. I had sworn to myself I was done with religion forever. When Hanukkah came, I simply refused to participate in the nightly prayers or in the lighting of the menorah. My father responded angrily by declaring I would, in that case, receive no Hanukkah presents. It was a tactical error on his part. I thought the no-presents rule was completely fair. I figured if I wanted to take a stand on principle, I had to be willing to pay the price. It was hard to watch my brothers receive expensive gifts for eight nights while I got none. But I would not surrender. In the end, it was my father who relented, giving me my presents all at once when the holiday was over. Another tactical error you might say, but it speaks to his natural generosity. He really did want to give good things to his children.

When he found me with my words-of-Jesus-in-red Bible, it was natural for him to assume that, having abandoned Judaism, I was now considering Christianity. I wasn't. Not then. I explicitly remember thinking, as I made my way through first the New Testament and then the Old, that the Bible could not, and must not, be believed. *Faith is the death of thought*, I told myself. As an aspiring intellectual, I intended to avoid it at all costs.

Still, in the very long run, all my father's fears were justified, so perhaps he knew me better than I knew myself.

The fact was, as a story—even leaving out the supernatural, *especially* leaving out the supernatural, taking it all as metaphor, I mean—the Bible made perfect sense to me from the very beginning.

I saw a God whose nature was creative love. He made man in his own image for the purpose of forming new and free relationships with him. But in his freedom, man turned away from that relationship to consult his own wisdom and desires. The knowledge of good and evil was not some top-secret catalogue of nice and naughty acts that popped into Eve's mind when a talking snake got her to eat the magic fruit. The knowledge was built into the action of disobedience itself: it's what she learned when she overruled the moral law God had placed within her. There was no going back from that. The original sin poisoned all history. History's murders, rapes, wars, oppressions, and injustices are now the inescapable plot of the story we're in.

The Old Testament traces one complete cycle of that history, one people's rise and fall. This particular people is unique only in that they're the ones who begin to remember what man was made for. Moses' revelation at the burning bush is as profound as any religious scene in literature. There, he sees that the eternal creation and destruction of nature is not a mere process but the mask of a personal spirit, I AM THAT I AM. The centuries that follow that revelation are a spiraling semicircle of sin and shame and redemption, of freedom recovered and then surrendered in return for imperial greatness, of a striving toward righteousness through law that reveals only the impossibility of righteousness, of power and pride and fall. It's every people's history, in other words, but seen anew in the light of the fire of I AM.

It made sense to me too—natural sense, not supernatural—that after that history was complete, a man might be born who could comprehend it wholly and re-create within himself the relationship at its source. His mind would contain both man and God. It made sense that the creatures of sin and history—not the Jews alone but all of us—would conspire in such a man's judicial murder. Jesus had to die because we had to kill him. It was either that or see ourselves by his light, as the broken things we truly are. It's only from God's point of view that this is a redeeming sacrifice. By living on earth in Jesus, by entering history, by experiencing death, by passing through that moment of absolute blackness when God is forsaken by God, God reunites himself with his fallen creation and reopens the path to the relationship lost in Eden. Jesus' resurrection is the final proof that no matter how often we kill the truth of who we're meant to be, it never dies.

I didn't think any of this was true, mind. That is, I didn't think it had actually happened. But I could see it was a completely cogent depiction of how a loving I AM would interact with a free humanity.

More important, in the years after I first read the Bible, as I struggled to educate myself and find my voice as a writer, the Bible story came to seem to me the story behind every story, especially the stories of the West. It was the way the Western mind understood itself. It was, as the poet William Blake said, "The Great Code of Art."

Being who I was, I tried to decipher that code in wholly material terms, the terms of the postmodern intellectual world, my world. As the years went on, I read *The Golden Bough* and learned to see the Gospels as a death-and-resurrection myth masquerading as history. I read the mythographers like Joseph Campbell and learned to understand the ways in which all such myths reflect the indescribable human experience. I read Freud and learned to see religion as a neurotic illusion, a projection of sexual complexes onto the universe. More and more, as I explored it, the endless meanings of the Bible obsessed me.

At the same time, all along I was struggling with my own worsening brokenness, my growing rage and my anguish. Searching for some meaning to my pain, I came to see Jesus' life as a mirror of my increasingly desperate search for enlightenment and inner peace. He was a storyteller; I was a storyteller. He suffered in agony; so did I. His story and my story became confused in my mind.

At last, when I was in my midtwenties, in that despair that does not know it is despair, I set about to write my magnum opus on the subject. I interwove the literary, mythical, psycho-sexual, and personal aspects of the gospel into a massive fictional retelling of Jesus' life, a novel I called *Son of Man*. The work—around six hundred typed manuscript pages when it was done—was meant to explain this Christ story completely, once and for all.

Alone in an empty room my wife and I could not afford to furnish, in semidarkness with the blinds drawn, I sat cross-legged on the floor, a fountain pen clutched in my hand, one notebook on my knees and the others spread around me. I scribbled the book in fevered bursts of inspiration page upon page, volume upon volume, hour after hour, day after day.

But by then, of course, I was already going mad.

CHAPTER 7

EXPERIENCE

I left home at seventeen, in anger and in pain.

By that time, my father and I had been fighting for years, often viciously. We shouted at each other. We slammed doors. We shook our fists. Once, I disparaged him so cruelly I made him cry. The battle was over my life, my future, most particularly my education.

The whole time I was growing up, the attitude toward education in my household was weird, complex, and contradictory. My family had learned to hold itself apart from the extravagant inelegance of *nouveau riche* Great Neck. The Cadillacs, the furs, the flash jewelry—we were superior to all that. We were in a class by ourselves. Fair enough, I guess. But at the same time, more subtly, we children had been taught to separate ourselves from the better aspects of the town's culture too.

All around us, there were aspirational second- and third-generation American Jewish kids looking to make good. Their parents had worked hard to rise into the upper-middle classes. It was the job of the children to keep rising through the traditional Jewish path of higher education. The sons and daughters of wholesalers and small-business owners would become doctors and lawyers. The sons and daughters of doctors and lawyers would become even more important doctors and lawyers—or senators and professors and executives and such.

But that sort of thinking was not for the likes of us Klavans, no, no. Striving, aspirational third-generation Jews? In need of education, guidance, and nurturing at the hands of teachers? Please! That image of us offended my mother and father both, though in different ways.

My mother did not want us to *rise* to a new social level, she wanted us to *be* at that level already. And what we could not be, she wanted us to seem. She was entranced by the trappings of upper-class WASP elegance. She wanted us to play tennis and wear blue blazers and smoke pipes, though presumably not all at the same time. But if she understood the ethos of hard work, study, risk, and sportsmanship that underlay such appearances, she never managed to communicate it to us—or at least to me— in any meaningful way. To me, it seemed that she wanted us to look and act like the classy guys in the tuxedo movies—instead of like the Great Neck Jews we were—but had no real concept of the substance beneath those flickering images.

In any case, my mother simply didn't have the force of personality to override my father's clamorous show-biz presence and point of view. And for him, education was just one more hurdle between you and success, one more hostile system that had to be gamed. He hadn't graduated college. And yes, on the one hand, he admitted this made him feel inferior to people who had. But on the other hand, he bristled when anyone suggested that a college education was valuable in and of itself. Sure, you needed that "piece of paper," to get ahead in life. But if you were proud of having a degree for its own sake, well, you were just a pretentious snob. What could you really learn from teachers, after all? Those failures! They couldn't even get a job in the real world, and they were jealous of anyone who could. Were you going to allow people like that to fill your head with information and opinions your own father never had? Did they think they were better than he was? Did you?

My parents were proud that my brothers and I were smart, that we read books and paid attention to culture. If nothing else, it was one more proof that we were superior to our neighbors. I can remember several times when one of my brothers or I referred to some highbrow novel around the dinner table. "Do you think anyone else in this neighborhood is discussing that book over dinner?" my father would ask triumphantly.

But the idea that our reading was just the first budding *sign* of intellect—the idea that we might need instruction from adults who had themselves studied and learned—no. My English teacher couldn't possibly know more about literature than I did. She was just a failed writer envious of my talents, another hostile obstacle to my success. We were all already smarter than she was. And not just smarter. More important: we were funnier. My father was a comedian, after all. When he called his sons *funny*, that was his highest praise.

And we were funny, my brothers and I, all four of us. When we weren't punching one another or holding one another's feet to the radiator or chasing one another around the room with the dog's chain or a kitchen knife or a dart from the basement dartboard, we were tearing one another to shreds with witty insults. It was brutal on the ego but, I have to admit, it was ceaselessly hilarious.

To my mind, looking back on it now, my mother's faux-elite snobbery and my father's narcissistic hostility made life too easy on us. If we were already better than everyone around us, we didn't have to compare ourselves to them or compete with their successes. If the world was hostile and envious of us, we didn't have to earn its respect. And if we were already smarter than our teachers, then no one could teach us anything. We never had to question our household opinions and points of view. We never had to put ourselves or our ideas to the test.

I rejected this worldview and I embodied it, both at once. I argued against it and I breathed it in. I read books and thought thoughts that my father found threatening and pretentious and, at the same time, I became antagonistic toward any outer authority. Especially, I became estranged from school to the point of open rebellion. I detested the place.

From elementary school on, I'd been conning my way through. Neglecting the work, getting by on native intelligence. Burdened every day with the fear of exposure. Hating the classroom because of the fear.

By the time I reached junior high, I had transformed this dysfunction into a philosophy just as my father had before me. I thought of school as nothing more than a bureaucratic roadblock on the path to life. I thought of teachers as my inferiors with no right to exercise authority over me. I thought of education as a scam, and I felt justified in scamming it right back. I did as little work as possible. I wrote my way around my ignorance of literature and history. I reasoned my way through math problems I didn't understand. I stumbled through science classes on luck and pluck. I don't think I ever cheated, but I wasn't above bluff and fakery and outright lying from time to time.

Once, after a chemistry class ended, my teacher summoned me to the front of the room. I knew what the problem was. The term was drawing to a close, and I hadn't yet handed in the final research paper that was going to supply a large percentage of our grade. I hadn't handed it in because I hadn't written it. I hadn't written it because I hadn't given it even two consecutive seconds of thought. The teacher had her grade book open in front of her on the desk, a pencil in her hand. She was going down the list of names in the book with the pencil point. "I don't seem to have received your paper yet," she said. I played startled. I reared back, wide-eyed. I said, "Really? But I handed it in two weeks ago!"

This was before computers, remember. There would have been only one copy of my paper. It couldn't have been easily reproduced. The teacher hesitated for a moment, scanning her records. Then she said, "Oh yes, here it is!" She'd actually found my grade! It was right there in her book! Somehow I had received an A-minus on a project I had never handed in. It's remarkable I still did not believe in God.

In English class, other lazy students got through by buying CliffsNotes, the little booklets that summarize the plots of classic novels and explain their themes so you can answer test questions without actually reading the novel itself. I didn't even have the time or energy to use these cheat sheets. Instead, I developed a technique that allowed me to convincingly pretend to have read any book without ever opening it. I discovered that if you delivered yourself of a radical negative opinion on a classic work of literature in a superior and knowing tone, no one ever questioned whether you had actually cracked the binding of the thing or not. If you declared that *Moby Dick* was a crashing bore; if you said *The Scarlet Letter* was overwritten and irrelevant; if you proclaimed *The Red Badge of Courage* was an act of literary fakery, the teacher's attention shifted from the novel itself to you, your brash eloquence, your haughty sophistication, the shock and cleverness of your position.[1] It never once occurred to anyone to put my knowledge to the test or make me support my point of view with specific examples.

Add to this sort of chicanery, my growing anger against authority—add to my anger the general insurrection of the sixties with all authority everywhere under attack and in retreat—and I was soon a hunkering teenage rebel. I was sullen, hard-drinking, often hungover, openly defiant of the rules. I tromped around in motorcycle boots and wore denim and leather, like some biker bandit in a B movie. I would passionately kiss and grope my girlfriends on the lawn outside and even mash them against the hall walls between classes.

Whenever a teacher or administrator scolded me for this, and more than once someone did, I would become enraged and aggressive, snarling in their faces.

I was thick across and muscular. I was only just growing out of my fighting phase. I was more intimidating than I realized. The male teachers would make threatening noises at me, but they never followed through. The female teachers learned to stay away. As for those two or three courageous souls, men and women both, who tried to talk to me, to help me—I wouldn't let them near. I did not trust them. I knew how my competitive father tried to sabotage my projects with his false mentorship. Why would some failure of a teacher be any different?

And yet all this while, I read and wrote. The beauty of prose mesmerized me. Making words into stories and characters gave me peace, like daydreaming onto the page.

But because I wouldn't accept anyone else's teaching, I could only learn more of what I already knew. My literary taste became cramped and limited. The intellectual values I'd developed in my boyhood hardened into small-minded prejudice. Toughness, cynicism, realism (a literary style that so often has nothing to do with reality), short, masculine Hemingwayan sentences—these were good. Idealism, faith, moral probity, beauty, high-minded Wordsworthian argument, and deep Faulknerian complexity—these were pretentious and bad. I had not read Wordsworth or Faulkner, of course. I didn't have to. Just dismissing them gave me a kind of power over them. That was the whole method of the con, even when I was conning myself.

These self-imposed restrictions on my taste not only skewed my education but also skewed my idea of what education was. The bluff, masculine, straightforward "good" writers I admired—Hemingway especially, but also Dashiell Hammett, Raymond Chandler, Jack Kerouac, and the like—played down whatever erudition they had. Only pretentious writers highlighted their educations. I disdained the novels of Faulkner and James Joyce on principle because they were blatantly literary, full of classical learning and erudite references. But the adventurer Hemingway, the private detective Hammett, the beatnik wanderer Kerouac, and World War soldiers like Chandler and Norman Mailer—they wrote about the streets, the battlefields, the road, the violent moment, real life. They had something much better than mere learning. They had *Experience*!

Experience! That's what made a writer great, I thought. Harsh, brutal, savage Experience—I would have done anything to get my hands on some. But where? There were nothing but lawns and homes and normal families around me as far as the eye could see.

I didn't want to go to war. Those in the know had declared the Vietnam conflict corrupt and evil. Patriotism was out of fashion. Warrior courage was out of fashion. The draft ended before I came of age and the war ended before I could have fought in it anyway. But, while I'm embarrassed to say it now, the truth is, the idea of joining up simply to serve my country in the armed forces never occurred to me. Where I came from, that was no part of the spirit of the age.

Instead, I took jobs whenever I could—not jobs that would teach me something or contribute to my future or my career. No, I took jobs that I hoped would get me nearer to the grit of things: Experience. I was a gas jockey, a warehouseman, a truck driver, a construction worker, a delivery boy to some of the dodgier areas of New York City. After seventeen years in grassy peace and comfort, I was hungry for anything that looked like cruel reality.

What I wanted most, though, was to wander. Not to travel—to drift. I had had wanderlust since I was a little boy. I never looked at rolling hills without yearning—aching—to walk to the top of the nearest one and see what was beyond it. My romantic fantasies often involved a girl in some other town, not this town. A brief affair. A tearful goodbye. Then, babe, I've got to travel on down that lonesome, dusty road.

These longings to roam were natural to me, but pop songs and novels and movies fed them with imagery. There was Ricky Nelson's ditty "Travelin' Man." It was a number-one hit when I was seven. Nelson sang of how he owned the heart of a girl in every port he passed through, from a "pretty Polynesian baby" to a "cute little Eskimo." I listened to that record until the grooves in the vinyl wore away. There was *Shane*—Jack Schaefer's classic western novella about a roving gunman who "rode into our little valley out of the heart of the great glowing West and when his work was done rode back whence he had come." It was my older brother's favorite novel for a while and I read it five times before I was twelve. And there was *Huckleberry Finn*. "I reckon I got to light out for the territory." He was a hero to me from my earliest days. My mother used to joke sometimes that I was a Jewish version of him: Huckleberry Fein. Then, when I was older, Jack Kerouac's *On the Road* stirred me to my heart. And Carole King's lovely drifter ballad "So Far Away."

When I was seventeen, I took a job at a gas station. I had just finished school and I wanted to earn money for my first road trip across the country. In those days before self-service pumps, an attendant used to fill your car, check your oil and tire pressure, and clean off your windshield with a squeegee and a rag. I was that guy. Six days a week, eleven hours a day, I ran to answer the bell that rang whenever a car drove into the station. I worked such long hours that at night, when I went to bed, I would hear the bell in my dreams and leap out from beneath the covers only to find myself standing in my bedroom, dazed. And every day, all day long, the radio in the gas station garage played that song, the season's big hit, "So Far Away." The wistful melody made me yearn for the highway with the force of erotic desire. For twenty years afterward, whenever I heard the opening bars, I could still smell gasoline—and I still hungered to be travelin' on.

Experience. That was the stuff of life and literature to me. A classical education was the last thing I wanted.

This was what my father and I fought about, more than anything. I had declared I would not go to college. Ironically, my father was panicked and enraged. All the years of my youth, he had denigrated teachers and intellectuals. Now I wanted no more part of them—and he was absolutely aghast. How would

I get a good job without that "piece of paper"? How would I get along in the world—that place he always called "reality"? But he didn't understand: I didn't want a good job. I was going to be a writer! I didn't need an education. I needed Experience.

In any case, I hated school too much to keep on going. I can't begin to describe my feverish contempt for the place. I despised classrooms. Sitting and sitting there, smothered by stopped time. I hated the fools and failures in authority. All the meaningless knowledge they wanted to saddle me with. I yearned for the world of Experience beyond the walls.

To put myself out of my misery, I volunteered for an experimental program. Students were allowed to fulfill the requirements of senior year with a mere eight weeks in summer school. I think the program was designed to clear the high school halls of juvenile delinquents. As I remember it, that's who showed up for the classes mostly: thugs, bullies, bad girls, and me. Spending the summer in school was excruciating. But then it was over. I was seventeen and I was free.

So I hit the road. For the next two or three years, off and on, I wandered. Back and forth across the country by car and Greyhound bus. Sometimes with a friend, often alone. Through wild storms and desolate summers. Through every state on the continent with the exception of North Dakota—I figured South Dakota stood in for both. I slept in hobo camps; in campgrounds; in public parks; in cheap, bug-ridden motels; and on a city sidewalk once or twice. I met people from the deep country, north and south, and from all the towns and cities along the way. Occasionally I had the sort of adventures I hungered for. A mudslide in Montana nearly hurled me and my car over a cliff. A blinding blizzard outside of Denver left me stranded and nearly frozen in a vast white wilderness off-road. A few times, I even met a girl here and there who let me live out some version of my pop-song fantasy: a brief, intense, meltingly romantic relationship and then, don't look twice, I was gone.

At some point during this first year of traveling, I did send out one college application. I don't remember why. Maybe I got bored between excursions. In any case, it was a careless, dashed-off thing. A quickly filled-in form. A quickly scribbled essay. I sent it to the University of California at Berkeley. It was the only college I thought I might enjoy. For one thing, it was as far away from home as I could get. If there had been a school floating out in the middle of the Pacific Ocean, I would have applied to that one too. But for another thing, Berkeley was where a lot of the riots took place during the sixties. Not just riots but drug use and wild sex too. That sounded like just the curriculum for me.

I didn't expect to get accepted. I didn't really care whether I got accepted or not. When I didn't hear anything back from the school, I assumed they had rejected me. But one day, in the midst of my ramblings, I found myself in San Francisco. Out of curiosity, I drove across the bay to the campus. I went into the admissions office and asked about my application. The lady there told me I had been accepted to the school, but they couldn't mail out my acceptance letter because I had not returned the padlock to my high school locker and would not officially graduate until I paid the high school a four-dollar fine!

This amused me no end. Not just the locker lock but the whole business, start to finish. Berkeley was considered one of the best universities in the country. Somehow, I had managed to fake my way into a top-flight school.

I decided, well, I would go.

CHAPTER 8

A MENTAL TRAVELER

I arrived in Berkeley and promptly fell into a pathological depression. Away from the endless arguments with my father, away from the mindless freedom of the open road, all that rage inside me turned in on itself.

I had talked my parents into paying for a tiny apartment on the city's north side. I didn't want to live in a dorm. I wanted privacy so I could go on writing four hours a day. I hated sitting in lecture halls, so I scheduled all my classes on Tuesdays and Thursdays. Even so, I rarely went to any of them. As a result, I was often isolated, cut off from much of college life.

The city itself was a disappointment to me. The radical years there were over. The riots and mayhem I'd been hoping to see had passed like a storm. The revolution of the sixties was supposed to have ushered in a new "Age of Aquarius" when all would be peace and love everywhere. Big surprise: it never happened. Instead, the college town's streets were littered with the detritus of the hoped-for millennium. Scruffy street people begged and sold drugs along the sidewalks of the main drag, Telegraph Avenue. Self-serious radicals hawked their failed philosophies with pamphlets and grandiose speeches in Sproul Plaza, the university quad.

Myself, I drank. I slept long hours, sometimes twelve, thirteen, fourteen hours a day. I caught colds that lasted for weeks and weeks. I haunted restaurants and bars, glum and beetle-browed, barely able to speak to strangers yet always looking to pick up girls. The few relationships I had with women were brief and reckless. When they were over, I would hole up in my room for days, tormented by hypochondriacal fears that I had contracted a sexual disease.

Late at night, through the night, I would write in a kind of fever. I would sit at the table by the window in my little kitchen. Week-old dirty dishes filled the sink beside me, the food on them turning green. I would scribble in my notebooks hour after hour without lifting my eyes. With a sort of mad discipline, I taught myself my trade. I would spend an entire night writing and rewriting a single sentence. Then I would spend the next night expanding the sentence into a paragraph and rewriting that. Then, during the next two nights, I would turn the paragraph into a page, writing and rewriting every word until it sang to me, enlarging that first line until I had a full scene or even a short story. When I was finished, I would stumble pale and grey into the pale, grey light of dawn. Dressed in a ratty trench coat, unshaven, hollow-eyed, I would wander down to the local doughnut shop to watch them make the first doughnuts of the day. I would carry a hot one home and devour it in a bite or two. Then I would crawl into bed and sleep and sleep until well into the afternoon.

After a couple of months like this, I finally realized something was wrong with me. I willed myself to get out of bed earlier and to get out of the apartment more. I joined the campus radio station as a news reader, just to meet people. I had an old friend from Great Neck in one of the dorms and he brought me into his weekly poker game. The worst of my depression started to lift, though a heavy sadness lingered in me still. I felt lost.

In class—when I did go to class—I went through all the usual razzle-dazzle shenanigans: bluff and fakery. I read none of the books. I conned and wrote my way to passing grades. I remember once in particular taking an essay test on William Blake's "Visions of the Daughters of Albion." It's a great poem—now one of my favorites of his—but I hadn't read a word of it at the time. Funnier still: Blake was both a poet and an engraver and the subject of the course was the interplay between the visual and written arts, so not only did I not know what "Visions" was about, I didn't even know whether it was a poem or a picture. I had to write the entire essay using the vaguest words I could think of so as not to give my ignorance away. "This work—if work is the word I want—draws a picture, so to speak, of Blake's internal world . . ." It was the utterest of utter nonsense. What poem or engraving doesn't draw a picture, so to speak, of the poet or artist's internal world? I laughed out loud when I received a grade of B-minus on the test. B-minus was fine with me. I just wanted to get by.

I should mention—for lovers of earthly justice—that I did get caught at this flim-flam once. It was incredibly humiliating. I took a seminar on the novels of William Faulkner, a small discussion group of maybe ten or twelve students. I was the star of the class. I had opinions on everything Faulkner had ever written. I would hold forth eloquently at almost every session. It was just the sort of bloviation with which I'd always hidden my ignorance, just the trick to avoid any sober fact-based discussion that might queer my con.

One day, however, the teacher sprang a short-answer quiz on us. She had warned us she would, and I tried to avoid it, but I mistook the schedule and got caught. It was awful. Here I'd been mouthing off about these books for weeks and I couldn't answer the simplest questions about their plots or characters—because, of course, I hadn't read them. I received an F on the test, and my fakery was revealed. Even worse, I had to go to the professor's office to pick up the test booklet personally. She was a smart, attractive woman whom I liked and respected. It was terrible to have to look her in the eye as she handed me the booklet, both of us knowing what a fraud I was. But if ever a son of Adam deserved his fate, I was that man!

By late winter of my first year in school, I felt as if I was strangling on my own wanderlust. Mardi Gras was coming to New Orleans. Now, there was a party town I'd always loved whenever I'd passed through it, all Dixieland, hookers, and booze. I bought a round-trip bus ticket. I put a hundred dollars cash in my pocket. I lighted out for the territory.

At first, it was spectacular. Mardi Gras was everything I

could have wished for. Even on the Greyhound down, a wild country girl in the seat beside me threw a blanket over us both and came into my arms in the deep shadows of the night. When I reached the city, I saw a full-blown Feast of Fools. Beneath the wrought-iron railings and lantern-style streetlights of the French Quarter, the people flowed and frolicked and danced. The crowds were so dense they carried me with them like a rip-tide. There were cold drinks and hot jazz, both of which I loved. There were grotesque floats carrying giant pagan gods made of papier-mâché. Half-naked men and women, their breasts draped with bead necklaces, their faces hidden behind masks, gamboled around the idols in an all-day Bacchanal. Local girls took me to their apartments. Drifter girls took me into their sleeping bags. I felt alive for the first time in half a year.

But by the third day, my money ran out. I had no credit cards. This was before ATMs. I had assumed I'd be able to cash a check, but no one would accept my identification. I had nowhere to stay, nowhere to clean up, not even a bag to sleep in. I spent one night in the basement of the stadium at Tulane University. The city had set the space aside to handle the influx of homeless wanderers. I slept on the concrete floor wrapped in my thin trench coat. When I woke up, my whole body was rigid and thrumming with cold. Another day, as I was swept along in the vast, roiling mob, I saw a girl lose her footing just ahead of me. I caught her arm to steady her. By some insane chance or providence, she turned out to be a girl from my high school! Reluctantly, she and her boyfriend let me sleep for a few hours on the spare bed in his dorm room.

After that, though, I was on the streets. The rains began, heavy tropical rains. I became as filthy and disheveled as all the other homeless drifters in the city. I had enough loose change in my pockets to buy rolls and doughnuts, but I was getting hungry too. When I tried to take shelter in the bus station for the night, the policeman there kept rapping me with his billy club whenever I dozed off. When I went out in the rain-drenched streets and curled up in a doorway, another cop dragged me to my feet and chased me away, threatening to put me in jail.

By the time the party ended, I was burning hot with fever. My vision was blurred. My mind was muddy. I staggered when I walked. All I had left in my pockets now was my ticket home. It took days to get a seat on one of the crowded buses out of town but I finally did it. I leaned my steaming forehead against the cool bus window and lapsed into semiconsciousness.

The bus rolled out. I grew sicker by the minute, by the mile. I coughed and shuddered and began to shiver uncontrollably. At a stop in Texas somewhere, an ancient-looking black man boarded the bus and sat down beside me. I was hallucinating by then, wandering lost in hazy dreams, but I'm pretty sure the guy was real. He saw me trembling next to him. He leaned over and felt my forehead. He took off his heavy overcoat and wrapped it around me, tucking it in behind my back and buttoning it closed under my chin. As the bus rolled on, he hand-fed me aspirins. He held a cup of water to my lips and steadied my head with his hand so I could drink. After I-don't-know-how-many hours of this treatment, my fever broke. I started pouring sweat.

"You'll be all right now, son," the man said to me. I fell into a deep sleep. When I woke up, I felt better—and the old man was gone. I was half-convinced he was an angel. If he wasn't then, he is now.

I made it back to school, but by the end of that academic year, I had had enough of it. I dropped out. I wandered around the country some more, then returned to Berkeley, where my friends were. I landed a job in the news department of a small radio station out by the bay. It was an ironic triumph. I went there to do a voice audition. I sat in the news director's office and read some news copy out loud. I'd never had a professional audition before. I was nervous. My reading was terrible and I knew it. I was sure I wouldn't get the job. As I came to the end of the copy, I glanced up. To my surprise, I saw a small picture of my father on the wall. It was a promotional football card with my father posing as a football player. Startled, I blurted out, "Hey, that's my dad!" The news director was from back east. He was a big Klavan and Finch fan. He hired me on the spot.

More Experience. Not long after I joined the station's small news team as a reporter, the newspaper heiress Patty Hearst was kidnapped from her Berkeley apartment by a gang of radicals. It was the crime of the decade. At nineteen, I found myself moving in a pack with the most famous reporters in the country. It was like some kind of crazy circus with journalists as the clowns. I saw sophisticated national newsmen get into fistfights at press conferences over who would put his camera where. I joined celebrity reporters in sneaking past watchful guards to get into crime scenes. I learned to steal documents off officials' desks like they did. At one point, a five-foot-nothing woman from some local newspaper somewhere taught me an excellent trick. As we walked together to a one-on-one interview with a police spokesman, she elbowed me in the solar plexus so hard she knocked me into a wall—just to make sure she got the interview first.

Meanwhile, the Patty Hearst story got curiouser and more deadly. Soon the missing heiress was issuing tape recordings announcing she had joined her kidnappers' radical army. She had herself photographed holding a machine gun during a bank robbery committed by her captors. Later, she claimed she had been brainwashed by them, but that didn't save her from doing time. It all climaxed down in Los Angeles with the radicals holed up in a house, shooting it out with the LAPD. The house caught fire and most of the radicals burned to death. So much for the Age of Aquarius.

By the time that final gunfight exploded, though, I had left the radio station and returned to university. I hadn't had a change of heart about school, not exactly. But a faint—the faintest—glimmer of understanding had begun to filter through the darkness of my angry and egotistical ignorance. It was beginning to seem to me just possible—just barely possible—that I did not know as much as I thought I did. It was beginning to occur to me that I might not learn what a really good writer needed to learn by staying out here in the working world. Experience was fine. Experience was fun. But no matter how much of it you got, you could only really experience the territory right around you, a vanishing arc of space and time. Not only that. Your personality shaped your perceptions of whatever you saw. Your upbringing, your culture, your little moment of history hemmed your vision round. In the words of my old pal William Blake—whom I still hadn't read yet—"The eye altering alters all."

But what if you could see what other men saw—"men and women too," as Blake would hurry to say? What if you could enter other minds? Not just those minds that shared your point of view, but also those that saw life differently, had other personalities, other upbringings in eras other than your own? What if you could become not just a Huckleberry rambler through the country you were given, not just a seeker of Experience in your accidental age but also, in Blake's mighty phrase, "a Mental Traveller" through a vast universe of deep and sometimes contradictory ideas?

Given my anger, given my egotism, given my ignorance, I'm not sure how such a notion had even begun to occur to me. But I think it had been suggested to my mind during that miserable first year in college by another old friend of mine: William Faulkner.

Here was an odd thing. Though I rarely read any of the work assigned in class, though I hardly ever studied for tests, I always bought every book that was listed on the syllabus and I never threw any of the books away. I was very conscientious about this. If the campus bookstore was missing a volume on my list, I would hunt it down elsewhere or order it and return to the store to pick it up when it arrived. Whatever books the school assigned, I bought them and kept them, completely unread. It was a strange thing to do, not like me at all. My little studio soon became lined, stacked, and littered with the many books I was ignoring.

So it happened one winter morning—late one winter morning after one of my long nights—I found myself lying awake in bed, bored and staring at the ceiling, too lazy to rise. I looked down over the blankets. One of the many books that were strewn around the room had come to be lying at the foot of the bed. My sleepy eyes focused on it. It was *The Sound and the Fury* by William Faulkner.

Now, as I've said, Faulkner was the sort of novelist I did not read. I didn't have to. I knew he was no good. Not tough. Not terse. Not realistic. He was florid and fancy and hard to understand. He made pretentious allusions that only pretentious intellectual snobs pretended to comprehend. I didn't have to look at a word he'd written to know that I disdained him utterly.

But here I was. Bored and snug in bed. *The Sound and the Fury* was the only book I could reach without getting out from under the blankets. So I curled around and snagged its cover between my fingertips and drew it to me. I figured if I actually read a page or two, it might give me a bit more credibility the next time I denounced the author. I scanned the first line.

Through the fence, between the curling flower spaces, I could see them hitting . . .

I read on. And wait, this wasn't hard to understand at all. It was a description of a golf game. If the writing was a little unclear, it was because the character describing the game was mentally retarded. And hey, that made sense. It was *The Sound and the Fury*, right? "A tale told by an idiot," like in that sound-and-fury speech from Shakespeare's *Macbeth*. I kept reading. The book told the same story four times from four different perspectives. That reminded me of something too. Oh, yes: the Gospels! I was beginning to see how this worked.

I read the book through to the end. I loved every page of it. And I loved Faulkner's *Light in August*. And I thought his *Absalom, Absalom* was one of the most profound and touchingly tragic novels I had ever read. I still felt I was betraying my values by admiring these fancy and elaborately written books. But I just couldn't help myself. I would've had to be blind to miss how good they were.

It took time, a long time, but the shock of discovering Faulkner began to edge me away from my deeply held and completely uninformed literary opinions. I began to experiment a little, reading other books that were somewhat different from what I usually enjoyed. Two of those books had a powerful effect on the way I experienced the intellectual atmosphere of the rest of my university days.

I went to college just as the ideas often called postmodernism were rising up through the educational system. Up to that time—under modernism—academics and intellectuals had considered themselves to be participating in a Great Conversation, an interchange carried on across the centuries by the major thinkers and artists of the Western canon. The idea was that by studying this conversation you could move closer to the Truth and so find a fuller wisdom about reality and what made for the Good Life. Now, though, those intellectuals who derided and even denounced the Western canon and Western values in general had come to the fore. Literature was no longer to be loved and learned from, but deconstructed to reveal its secret prejudices and power plays. Language itself was now considered not a rude tool for transmitting meaning but a political instrument of imperialism and oppression that needed radical criticism. The very idea of Truth was being rejected. All morals were relative, all cultures equally legitimate.

Those professors who had studied literature under the old system were on the defensive and had lost their confidence. I remember sitting in a class on Alfred Lord Tennyson, a poet of the highest genius who often comes under attack now for his Victorian values. The professor was lecturing to an auditorium full of students about *The Charge of the Light Brigade*. The poem is a brilliant description of a disastrous but courageous charge on a Russian cannon emplacement by six hundred British cavalrymen in 1854 during the Crimean War.

> *Theirs not to make reply,*
> *Theirs not to reason why,*
> *Theirs but to do and die:*
> *Into the Valley of Death*
> *Rode the six hundred.*

The professor, a mild-mannered woman in her forties, was discussing the poem with gentle enthusiasm when a very serious young lady in a very serious pair of spectacles rose from one of the front seats and demanded angrily, "How can we even read this poem when all it does is glorify war?"

The poor professor's face went blank. Clearly, she was a product of the old school. She studied literature because she loved literature not because she wanted to use it to preen herself on her own political virtue. She had never had to defend the beauty of beauty before, or the wisdom of wisdom. She smiled, embarrassed. She shrugged weakly. "I see what you mean," she said.

At the back of the auditorium, I leapt to my feet, appalled. Here was a poem I had actually read—and I loved it. I still do. Because it's great. Inarticulate with passion, I began to slap my open volume of Tennyson with the back of my hand, reading the opening lines aloud and saying, "Listen! Listen to this! Listen! 'Half a league, half a league, half a league onward—all in the valley of Death rode the six hundred.' You can hear the horses! You can—listen!—you can feel the courage and the madness, everything, it's all there . . ." I babbled on like that for a few more seconds and then dropped back into my seat, blushing, feeling like an idiot.

The professor made a bland gesture in my general direction as if to say, "Yes . . . yes . . . I suppose it's something of that sort," and then continued with her lecture. Such survivors from the old days could raise no defense against the postmodern onslaught.

Myself, I could see the logic behind postmodernism and its moral relativism. Much of what we think is good—individual freedom, equality before the law, tolerance for conflicting opinions—is learned from Western culture and taken on faith. Why should we not accept that other cultures with other values and other faiths might be just as legitimate as our own? I could see the logic—and yet, my senses rebelled. To abandon those basic principles seemed false to something equally basic within me. It seemed an act of violence against my idea of what a human being was. I was torn between the intellectual fashion of the day and my own deepest convictions.

That's part of the reason why *Hamlet* obsessed me so: it was the story of a man who could not decide what was right, what was true. I read it first in a Shakespeare course, then read it again and again and watched many of the movie versions too. One scene—the "mad scene"—haunted me endlessly. Hamlet is pretending to be insane—and may actually be a little insane at that point. When he's asked what he's reading, he answers weirdly, "Words, words, words." He talks about how his internal moods seem to transform outer reality so that he can never be sure what the world is really like. Morality especially has come to seem to him completely dependent on his own opinions. "There is nothing either good or bad, but thinking makes it so," he says.

How wild was this? Shakespeare had predicted postmodernism and moral relativism hundreds of years before they came into being! Like Hamlet, the postmodernists were declaring that language did not describe the world around us. It was just "words, words, words." Like Hamlet, the postmodernists announced that what we thought was reality was just a construct of our minds that needed to be disassembled in order to be truly understood. And like Hamlet, the postmodernists had dismissed the notion of absolute morality. "There is nothing either good or bad, but thinking makes it so."

But there was one big difference. Hamlet said these things when he was pretending to be mad. My professors said them and pretended to be sane. Shakespeare was telling us, it seemed to me, that relativism was not just crazy, it was *make-believe* crazy, because even the people who proclaimed it did not believe it deep down. If, after all, there is no truth, how could it be true that there is no truth? If there is no absolute morality, how can you condemn the morality of considering my culture better than another? Relativism made no sense, as Shakespeare clearly saw.

But what was the answer then? On the one hand, it seemed prejudiced and dogmatic to cling to moral absolutes. On the other hand, relativism was self-contradictory, mad-scene gibberish. As a writer who wanted to describe reality, how could I steer between the craziness of postmodernism and the rigidity of self-righteous self-certainty?

The seed of the answer was planted in me by Fyodor Dostoevsky's novel *Crime and Punishment*. I was about twenty when I read it. It changed my life. I had moved out of Berkeley by then and was commuting to my classes from across the San Francisco Bay. I had a dingy little apartment on one of the pretty city's pretty hills, a street of townhouses with bay windows, the cable-car bells ringing in the near distance. I still didn't do much schoolwork, but I read more of the books

I bought now, and read a broader range of books than ever. I had learned how to turn off my ever-so-insistent opinions and simply let the authors speak to me. I had learned to ride a story like a wave, wherever it went.

This was an important change in me, an essential change. Stories are not just entertainment, not to me. A story records and transmits the experience of being human. It teaches us what it's like to be who we are. Nothing but art can do this. There is no science that can capture the inner life. No words can describe it directly. We can only speak of it in metaphors. We can only say: it's like this—this story, this picture, this song. I had finally sloughed off some of my teenage arrogance and started to listen to those descriptions with an open mind. Without knowing it, I had joined the Great Conversation.

So . . . I remember sitting in my San Francisco apartment one evening, sitting in a rickety, straight-backed wooden chair at my little writing desk. The paperback of *Crime and Punishment* was open like a prayer book in my two hands, held under the desk lamp. The lamplight was dim. I had to stare at the small print on the page through the deepening dusk. I stared, my eyes wide, my lips parted. I read.

Crime and Punishment is the story of Raskolnikov, a former college student. Sunken-eyed, feverish, half-crazed, depressive, he reminded me of me when I first arrived at school. Raskolnikov comes to believe that morality is relative, that a great man can create his own right and wrong in the name of freedom and power. In the grips of that belief, he commits two horrific axe murders. Then, too late, he discovers he has violated the absolute moral law within himself. It was real all along, much more real than he knew. His conscience will not let him rest. He is tortured by remorse. But slowly, he comes under the sway of a Christian girl who has fallen into prostitution. Through her love and kindness and faith, Raskolnikov begins to accept his sinfulness and shame and to return to the moral world. As the story ends, he begins the "new story" of his redemption in the Gospels.

When I finished the book, I laid it down on the desktop, my hand unsteady. I pressed the heels of my palms against my forehead as if to keep my thoughts inside me. After reading that novel, I was never quite the same. I did not accept the Christian aspect of it then. I couldn't. It was too alien to my upbringing, too at odds with the mental atmosphere in which I lived. I told myself that Dostoevsky was merely using Christ as a symbol for the reality of moral truth. But never mind. I knew beyond a doubt that the essential vision of the novel was valid. The story's *rightness* struck me broadside so that the journey of my heart changed direction. From the moment I read *Crime and Punishment*—though I did not know it, though it took me decades, though I was lost on a thousand detours along the way—I was traveling away from moral relativism and toward truth, toward faith, toward God.

Soon after this, I met Ellen, the woman who would become my wife. I'll tell all about that in the next chapter, but for now, I want to end with this.

Ellen's father, Thomas Flanagan, was the chairman of the Berkeley English department. This had nothing to do with how I met her. I was so mentally dissociated from the school experience that I had no idea what the chairman of an English department was. But moving in with Ellen turned out to be sort of like marrying the boss's daughter. Even the professors who suspected me of faking it started to give me As. It's probably how I got my degree.

More importantly, Ellen's father and mother took to me. The first time I came into their house, I was approached by their yapping wire-haired terrier. I laughed and said, "Asta!" Asta was the dog in Dashiell Hammett's *The Thin Man*—a schnauzer in the novel but a wire-hair in the famous 1934 film. Tom's face lit up when I called the dog that name. I think both he and Ellen's mother were thrilled their daughter had finally brought home a boyfriend who might have actually once read a book! In any case, they kindly welcomed me into their family.

It was a fine, delightful irony. Here I was, an academic fraud, suddenly attending dinners and cocktail parties with the stars of the university's English department. These were brilliant men, almost all men, a faculty rated second in the country only to Yale's. They spoke effortlessly and allusively of literature from Homer to Seamus Heaney. Seamus himself was a good friend of Tom's and sometimes in the house. He and Tom and Ellen and I even traveled through Ireland together once, the Irish poet and the Irish-American professor-novelist discoursing on the history of every blade of grass. These men—all these learned men I met—seemed to know everything about everything. They made casual jokes about lines from poems I had never heard of. They discussed current events in the context of a history I only dimly understood. They lived, in other words, in a world whose existence I had only just begun to suspect: the world of ideas. For the first time, I started to wonder whether it might be my world, the world I belonged in.

So just as my years at university were ending, I was coming to understand what an education was. To escape from the little island of the living. To know what thinking men and women have felt and seen and imagined through all the ages of the world. To meet my natural companions among the mighty dead. To walk with them in conversation. To know myself in them, through them. Because they are what we've become. Every blessing from soup bowls to salvation they discovered for us. Individuals just as real as you and me, they fought over each new idea and died to give life to the dreams we live in. Some of them—a lot of them—wasted their days following error down nowhere roads. Some hacked their way through jungles of suffering to collapse in view of some far-off golden city of the imagination. But all the thoughts we think—all the high towers of the mind's citadel—were sculpted out of shapeless nothing through the watches of their uncertain nights. Every good thing we know would be lost to darkness, all unremembered, if each had not been preserved for us by some sinner with a pen.

I wanted to read their works now, all of them, and so I began. After I graduated, after Ellen and I moved together to New York, I piled the books I had bought in college in a little forest of stacks around my tattered wing chair. And I read them. Slowly, because I read slowly, but every day, for hours, in great chunks.

I pledged to myself I would never again pretend to have read a book I hadn't or fake my way through a literary conversation or make learned reference on the page to something I didn't really know. I made reading part of my daily discipline, part of my workday, no matter what. Sometimes, when I had to put in long hours to earn a living, it was a rough slog. I still remember the years when I would wake up at 3:00 a.m. to go to a job writing radio news for the morning rush hour. I would come home from a seven-hour shift and play with my baby daughter. Then I would write fiction for four hours. Then, finally, I would read—my eyes streaming with tears of exhaustion—read until past midnight even if it meant I'd get only an hour or two of sleep before I woke up at three and went to work again.

The stacks around my wing chair dwindled and I built them up again and they dwindled again and I built them up.

It took me twenty years. In twenty years, I cleared those stacks of books away. I read every book I had bought in college, cover to cover. I read many of the other books by the authors of those books and many of the books those authors read and many of the books by the authors of those books too.

There came a day when I was in my early forties—I remember I was coming out of a pharmacy on the Old Brompton Road in London—when it occurred to me that I had done what I set out to do. I had taught myself the culture that had made me. I had taught myself the tradition I was in. In the matter of personal philosophy, I had finally earned the right to an opinion. I was no longer what I had been in my youth.

Against all odds, I had managed to get an education.

CHAPTER 9

LODESTAR

My last year in college, I owned an ancient jalopy, a maroon Dodge Dart. My friends and I christened it the Artful Dodge, after Oliver Twist's pickpocket pal the Artful Dodger. Because I had moved into San Francisco, I had to drive the Artful Dodge across the Bay Bridge to the Berkeley campus on the days when I had classes. A pal of mine who didn't own a car let me park the Dodge in his assigned space in the garage of his apartment building.

One day in early Autumn, I was walking back from campus to collect the car for the drive home. I looked up from my usual reverie and saw a woman hitchhiker standing across the street. She was slender and tall—as tall as I am—and as beautiful as a model on a magazine cover. To this day I remember the words that went through my head when I first saw her: *My God, would you look at that gorgeous Amazon!*

She was gorgeous—and she was literally asking to be

picked up! Standing in the cross street by the parked cars with her thumb out, trying to flag a ride. I knew it wouldn't be long before some other guy saw her and swept her away. In fact, I was sure it was going to happen at any moment. And there I was, still half a block from where the Artful Dodge was parked.

I started running. I've always been fast on my feet and I reached the garage and my car in only a few seconds. I unlocked the Dodge, tossed my schoolbooks inside, and slid behind the wheel. The Artful was a good old car, it really was, but it never started on the first turn of the key, not ever. It was old. Most times when I tried to get it going, it wheezed; it coughed; it stuttered; it only started on the third or fourth try.

But this day of all days, the Dodge roared to life on the instant. I wrestled the transmission stick on the steering wheel and threw the car into reverse. The tires screamed on the concrete as I shot the car backward out of its space, spun it round right, and then fired it out of the garage like a bullet—a wobbly, rattling, dirty, maroon bullet.

The streets of Berkeley in that neighborhood were laid out in a one-way grid. The Gorgeous Amazon Hitchhiker was to my right but the road outside the garage ran leftward only. I would have to go all the way around the corner to get back to her—and so I did, rocketing insanely through a busy residential area at about fifty miles an hour. I wove in and out of traffic. I skirted pedestrians. I have one vivid memory of a gray-haired lady with a shopping bag dangling from her wrist, frozen in my windshield, her face agape with terror. I somehow managed to swerve around her and go racing past. It's possible I screamed at her some words I shouldn't have.

But at last, I saw the hitchhiker up ahead with only one car between us. I could make out that the driver of that car was male, and while I didn't pray for him to go blind or die, I confess I did try to seize hold of his mind with my own and direct his thoughts away from any idea of stopping. To my astonishment, this appeared to work. The Gorgeous Amazon went on standing in the road with her thumb out and the guy in front of me drove right past her.

I pulled up alongside her. Trying to keep my voice steady and to dull what I knew must be the insane glaze of my rolling stare, I worked down my window and ever-so-casually asked if I might offer the lady a lift. I remember full well the sensation I had when she sat down in the front seat beside me. Nothing like a surge of passion. Nothing like a soundless symphony of invisible violins. It was instead almost exactly like what you feel when you are doing a jigsaw puzzle, when you have been searching for a piece without success for a long time, and suddenly you pick the right one from the pile and fit it to the picture with a whispered click.

"Sharp short," she said to me. Meaning: *nice car.*

"We call it the Artful Dodge," I told her.

She thought I was married because I used the word *we.* I thought my whole life made a kind of sense it had never made before.

I drove her back to her place, a house in the hills where she rented a room. I went inside with her and we sat and talked for more than three hours. I was so afraid she would see the way I felt about her—how gone I was—that I lost my nerve and couldn't bring myself to ask for her phone number. *I'll always be able to find her house again*, I told myself as I drove home. But in the days that followed, I found it wasn't so. Her house was hidden among the mazes of winding lanes up there. *Well,* I thought, after searching for it fruitlessly, *I'll go back to the place where she hitchhiked and find her there.* But her car, broken that first day, had been repaired soon after. She wasn't hitchhiking anymore.

Every day then, at the same hour each day, I would drive by the spot where I had first seen her, but she was never there. Even on days when I had no classes, I would travel across the bay to look for her. By then, I had begun to realize in some callow way what had happened to me, what a stroke of luck, or gift of providence it was. I knew I would find the Amazon again eventually, because I knew I had to.

After a few weeks of searching, though, I began to grow desperate. I considered phoning her father. She had mentioned he was the chairman of the English department, whatever that meant. I looked him up in the school directory and, yes, there he was. It was a daunting thought—to call up a professor and ask him to help me find his daughter for libidinal purposes—but I was ready to do it.

Fortunately, before it came to that, I managed to stumble on the girl herself. I was on one of my passes by her old hitchhiking place when I spotted her walking to her car, which was parked nearby. I pulled up beside her and asked her out. Within weeks we were living together in an apartment in San Francisco. Four years later we were married. We're married still.

My marriage to Ellen has not been an ordinary one, not by a long shot. It has been a lifelong romance. I love her, by which I mean her good is my good and her misfortune mine, and I love her passionately, by which I mean I hunger for her company as well as her touch. This has not changed even a little in our nearly forty years together. In nearly forty years, we have had exactly one quarrel. It was a meaningless flair of temper more than thirty years ago. Our apartment was being painted. Everything was in chaos. I had a night job and hadn't slept in weeks. We were both out of sorts, and we snapped at each other. It quickly passed. For the rest, we have been poor and rich together, crazy and sane, happy and miserable, but never wholly out of harmony. I find I can no longer even dream a woman who is not in some sense she.

But more than that. Our marriage has taken on a life of its own. It has become a third creation, greater than anything we are individually or together. I like to think we're perfectly decent people, Ellen and I, but I have all the usual flaws of men and she of women. We're clearly neither one of us as special as this vessel that contains us. Our marriage shines around us and between us with an otherly light, a sacred habitation for our shambolic humanity. It is soul stuff made visible.

Living within such a spiritual sanctuary has an effect on you over the years. Just knowing such a marriage can exist refashions the way you look at life. For me, it put limits on what I could call illusory or meaningless. Other men could believe that subjective experience is by nature relative and unreliable. Other men could reason from suffering to nihilism. Not me. Our marriage gave undeniable substance to the inner experience of true love, and true love in turn shone a light on the redemptive possibilities even of tragedy. Even the kingdom of evil came to seem to me like only the empty space where true love might have been. And when, over time, I had reasoned my way to God, it was our marriage, in part, that made me trust my reasoning. I trusted myself because I had recognized love when I saw it, and it was the fact of our long love that had slowly revealed to me a greater love than ours, the love that was our love's source and inspiration. It was as if our marriage had guided me through my days from a realm beyond the ordinary, the way a lodestar shines from deepest space yet nonetheless leads you home.

All this would only dawn on me and shape me over the course of decades. At the start, our relationship was mostly what these things are: sex and giddiness and setting up house. I met Ellen at a good time in my life, even a jolly time, relatively speaking. The depression and anger that had marked my first year at school had receded. Bumming around the country and working at the radio station had fed a little of that hunger for Experience that bedeviled me so much. I was glad to be back at school and, if I was still more or less vamping my way through higher education, I was also beginning to discover what I needed and wanted to learn. I was living in San Francisco, a lovely city. I was dating several girls whom I liked. Things were going all right for me. Finding Ellen just seemed like the natural next step in a good life.

But I think I already knew that the good life wouldn't continue. I think I already knew, deep down, that something was wrong with me. That depression I'd experienced my first months at school: now that I'd gotten some distance from it, I could look back and see it had been a really bad business. The long sleeps and the heavy drinking, the endless fevers and sunken-eyed solitude. Once you have felt that tide of darkness rising in you, you always know it might rise again.

It did rise from time to time, not full-blown depression maybe, but sorrow for no reason; anger for no reason; ugly, tormenting thoughts and a mood of persistent, unshakable melancholy. I called it the Bola—after that string with a weight on each end that some South American Indians used to use for a throwing weapon—because it seemed to come out of nowhere and wrap itself around my throat, growing tighter and tighter until I felt it would strangle me. Sometimes I thought it was connected to the writing process. The Bola would often hit me as I was finishing a book and I would wonder if my subconscious was punishing me for succeeding at something when I knew my father wanted me to fail. Other times, though, it seemed to just be there, inside me, less like a bola, really, than like an ensnaring interior spider web, interwoven strands of rage and sorrow and twisted sexual fantasies and imaginary arguments with my parents that would replay in my brain obsessively.

When I graduated college, Ellen and I moved to Manhattan. We found an apartment on the west side, a tiny place but in a nice neighborhood and renting cheap. My parents gave me a little money to start my life with, enough so I didn't have to get a job right away. Ellen continued college at Barnard. I began to try to sell the last novel I'd written and to write a new one. In both enterprises, I was hampered by the fact that I had no idea what I was doing, and no one who could explain it to me.

I had no mentor. I had never had a mentor, only an anti-mentor in my father. I had had no one—no one I trusted—to teach me even the simplest things about starting out in life, or beginning a career. I did not know there was such a thing as a career. I did not know that you could expect to move through it in stages, to learn from your failures and build upon your successes. I did not know that you could seek advice and help from older people. In fact, my father had left me so leery of authority, I wouldn't have dreamed of consulting my elders about anything. To me, they all seemed like bitter and crafty competitors out to trip me up.

I did not even know about the virtues of hard work. This seems almost unbelievable to me now, but it's true. My father had taught me that talent was like a delicate mechanism that would break or wear out from overuse. I was a hard worker by nature. I worked hard when I was working certainly; I crafted every sentence with care and went over it and over it. But I did not know that you could wake up earlier and accomplish more; that you could work weekends if you had to; that you could strive to achieve not just excellence but also prosperity and that the two need not be in conflict. I didn't know anything about anything really and I did not have anyone who could teach me.

The new novel I began to work on was called *Face of the Earth*. It was, if I say so myself, an excellent idea for a story. Inspired by my wanderings around the country, it concerned two young drifters, a wan intellectual type and a brash braggart. The braggart spins a yarn that may or may not be true about his pursuit of a woman who may or may not exist. In trying to get at the truth of the story, the intellectual not only falls in love with the woman in the braggart's story but begins to suspect that the braggart murdered her. It was a good plot. It was meant to deal with my thoughts on storytelling, with the difficulty of distinguishing reality from narrative, and with the way sexual desire sweeps us into the greater life and death of nature. It suffered from lyrical writing and a lot of youthful mythological symbolism—and from the fact that I still often worked late at night into early morning. It's a terrible time to write. Every awful word you put down seems like a masterstroke. Still, all that said, the book was a leap for me, the best thing I'd written up to that point.

As for selling my previously completed novel, the last book I'd written while in college . . . well, I knew I needed an agent but I didn't have the first clue how to find one. Instead of writing polite query letters the way you're supposed to, I went around the city barging unannounced into agents' offices with my boxed manuscript under my arm. I would explain how talented I was to whomever would listen, then demand that the agent read my work. Receptionists gaped at me in comical shock. Some of the top agents in New York actually came out of their offices to see me out of pure curiosity. One guy took me by the elbow and virtually hurled me out into the hall, shouting after me, "This isn't how it's done!" In spite of him, I actually did find an agent this way eventually, but she couldn't sell the book anywhere.

My money began to run out. I took odd jobs and managed to sell an article here and there for added cash, but I couldn't stretch out my funds forever. I became frustrated and the tide of depression began to rise in me again.

The city, meanwhile, was in a tailspin. The serial killer Son of Sam was terrorizing the public. I sold an article about the effects of his attacks, interviewing some of the trauma-tized friends of his victims. I can still remember their shocked and gutted gazes. The sight of them never left me. A winter of brutal cold had given way to a summer of relentless heat. Puerto Rican nationalists were disrupting the workday with bomb threats. Ellen was forced to come home from her sum-mer job more than once when her building was shut down.

On my twenty-third birthday, July 13, the metropolis was plunged into darkness during a citywide blackout. Ellen and I had saved up painfully for a special birthday dinner in a fancy restaurant. We were eating when I glanced out the front win-dow and saw a cascading shadow wipe the brilliance from the skyline. The restaurant management strove to keep the cus-tomers happy by handing out free wine in the dark. Poor as we were, we were only too eager to take advantage of the offer. Riots and looting were breaking out in the northern slums, but it was quiet enough where we were. As the blacked-out city burned around us, we went dancing home together along the sidewalk with me singing "They All Laughed" at the top of my lungs.

One of the local tabloids ran a cartoon soon afterward that showed the island of Manhattan sinking into the harbor while businessmen paddled for shore on their briefcases. That was pretty much how I felt about the city. New York can be a wonderful town, but it's never really suited me. Too much stone; too much noise; not enough opportunity for solitude. I wanted out. I was relieved when my older brother helped me land a job on a newspaper in a bureau in the rural exurbs, a hundred miles away. Ellen had graduated college by then, so we moved north. We took up residence in a gatekeeper's cottage on an estate. It was little more than a shack really, but it was up on a hill with a view of a horse paddock and the fields beyond. I loved it there.

I loved newspaper work too: the excitement and, of course, the Experience. Working the county's small towns, I got to cover every kind of story from murders to political shenanigans to the occasional county fair.

One morning I was sitting in the run-down, smoke-filled cubicle that was the bureau's office just off the main street of the county seat. I heard a call come in over the fizzling police radio that sat on top of an old filing cabinet. I rushed out the back door into the parking lot, jumped into my elderly Volvo, and raced to the scene. I got there just in time to see state troopers and sheriff's deputies carrying the body of a young woman out of the woods. She had been hitchhiking, just as my Ellen once had.

The police caught her killer quickly. It turned out he was the boyfriend of one of the richest girls in town, the wayward daughter of a local horse breeder. She lived with her lover in a house on her dad's vast estate. Her friends on the estate knew the guy was creepy. They'd begged her to break up with him, but she wouldn't do it. She liked the fact that the relationship made her father angry. At one point, desperate, her friends had called the newspaper—called me specifically. The boyfriend had been arrested for exposing himself in the local pornographic bookstore. They wanted me to write about it. They hoped that seeing the story in the paper would bring the girl to her senses. It wasn't news, so I couldn't run it. Too bad. Eventually, the horse breeder's daughter and her crazy boyfriend had a quarrel. He stormed off and took his anger out on the hitchhiker, beating her to death. It was a story straight out of Raymond Chandler.

The horse breeder was eager to avoid being connected to the murder. The powerful head of a prominent family, he turned to the county sheriff for help. The sheriff was a dour man, who hated nothing so much as the local press. He was only too willing to protect the horse breeder from any pesky and intrusive reporters, namely me. He ordered that roadblocks be set up, manned by deputies in patrol cars, blocking every entrance to the horse breeder's sprawling estate. No one could get through without being identified by the deputies. And no one on the farm was answering the phone.

There was, however, a young woman working for the Sheriff's Department who had taken a liking to me. We used to chat with each other over the pinball machine in the local diner. One night soon after the murder, as I was sitting alone in the bureau, the phone rang. When I answered, a woman's voice said, "Step out the back door. A black car will pull up. Get in the backseat." I hung up the phone. I laughed out loud. I thought, *I've been waiting to get a phone call like that my whole life!* I felt as if I had actually become Philip Marlowe. Experience!

Sure enough, when I stepped out the back door into the parking lot, the woman from the Sheriff's Department drove up in a long black car. When I got in the backseat, she instructed me to lie down on the floor. I fitted my body uncomfortably over the drive shaft tunnel and she covered me with a blanket, head to toe. Then, with me hidden from view, she drove past the sheriff's roadblocks up to the horse farm. I sat with the horse breeder's daughter's friends and they told me the whole story of her ill-fated romance. The next morning, it was splashed all over our front page. The sheriff was furious. I loved newspaper work.

But it was an all-consuming job, morning to midnight. For the first time in years, I was unable to write fiction every day. The most disturbing thing about this was how happy it made me. Getting out of the house, working an interesting job, being with colleagues I liked, making money—these things gave me enormous pleasure, as they would any young man. The newspaper forced me to realize that writing novels, the work I knew I was born for, was not good for me, psychologically speaking.

The writing life is brutal on a wounded mind. It really is. So much time spent alone. So much time spent in self-reflection.

Emotional wounds heal in other people's hearts but you have to reopen yours and examine them in order to re-create their painful feelings on the page. Ugly, twisted, vicious thoughts flitter through other people's minds, but you have to seize yours and hold them to the light in order to understand the soul's shadowy corners. You have to shred your comfortable pieties. You have to tear your illusions to feathers and rags. When you're working well, you become bad company, inward-turning, querulous, obsessed. There are plenty of harder jobs, I know. Homemakers, soldiers, cops, firemen, laborers—they all put in tougher days than writers do. But the writing life, so help me, could drive even a sane man crazy. If you're half crazy already, as I was, it will drive you completely out of your mind. It was healthy for me to be away from it.

I should have stayed away. I should have enjoyed the time. I should have put in a few years, five years, say, as a journalist. I could have learned more about politics, crime, and business from the inside. Established a reputation. Then I could have written a novel—probably a better novel than I was capable of at the moment. I just couldn't do it that way, though. Again, I was so ignorant of how a career works, how a life works. My father had always told me that a writer who takes a job will never get around to writing. One day, he'll wake up and he'll be sixty-five with a gold watch for retirement and an unfinished novel in his desk drawer. Writers write, Dad always said; and if you're not writing, you're not a writer. I sort of half understood that this was more of his bad advice—why he presumed to know anything about it at all, I can't say—but the idea frightened me nonetheless. As much as I loved the news-paper, every day I spent there felt to me like another day closer to that gold watch and failure.

Then my girlfriend sold my novel. Ellen had taken a sec-retarial job at a literary agency in Manhattan. She asked her bosses if she might send *Face of the Earth* around to publishers and they said yes, go ahead. To everyone's surprise, including mine, she got an offer on the book—a tiny offer but from one of the most famous editors at one of the best literary houses in town. With a check for a hot $7,500 in my hand, I did what any mentally unbalanced young writer would do under the circumstances: I quit my job and began to plan my next novel.

That was pretty stupid, but I did something else at the same time. I married Ellen—and that may have been the single best idea I ever had.

We'd been living together for four years. My original sense that we were interlocking pieces in some cosmic jigsaw puzzle had never left me. I didn't think much of ceremonies and rituals, of course. They were relics of an outmoded past, and I was far above such things. But I agreed to a gathering of about a dozen family members and friends at the cottage, and a few quick words from a preacher out on the lawn. It drizzled all that day. But just before the ceremony was due to begin, the rain stopped and a single golden beam of sunlight shone down on the spot by the willow tree where the cere-mony was to take place. Ellen and I stood together in that light while a minister from a Unitarian church pronounced us man and wife. "We gather together in the presence of that power whom some people call God and others call nature and for whom some have no name at all . . . ," he said. "The Church of Amorphous Rambling," one of my brothers called it.

The moment the service was over, however, I realized I had been wrong, utterly wrong. It struck me full force right away: the ceremony *did* matter. It was like a living story representing a truth that could not be otherwise told. It changed something in me on the instant. It created a mysterious but tremendous difference in the relationship between my girl and me.

I left the lawn. I walked back into the cottage. I went into the bathroom and closed the door. I looked at myself in the mirror, a married man. Dazed but euphoric, I raised my hand and gave myself the high sign: thumb and forefinger curled together into an *o* for *okay*!

I was a fool in so many ways and really half insane by then. But somehow—and not for the last time in my life—I had managed to stumble into the great good thing.

CHAPTER 10

GOING CRAZY

Our wedding day—then our honeymoon in Italy—were just about the last happy days I would have for the next four years.

The publication of *Face of the Earth* was a disaster. My famous editor was a brilliant and courtly gentleman but also a raging drunk. When he invited me to his apartment so we could go over the manuscript together, I was thrilled—until I saw the shambling, quivering wreck of a man he became in his off hours. Before the book made it to the stores, he left the publishing house and went into rehab. Without the famous editor to shepherd my novel into the world, it was universally ignored. The blow to my already fragile ego was so catastrophic I didn't even feel it. I simply buried the broken pieces of myself in comforting and increasingly grandiose fantasies.

These fantasies had been growing in me over the years, winding round my mental life like cobwebs and vines. The darker my internal world became, the more I soothed myself by hunkering within these dreams. My father's caustic and belittling voice had become an inner voice to me now, and to counter it I developed a defiantly overblown sense of myself, a brittle narcissism not unlike his own. This grandiosity even crept into my prose style. I had tried hard to teach myself to write sentences that were clean and clear, but now my work was becoming flowery and pompous. My ambitions grew flowery and pompous too—cosmic; impossible. I'm sure this was not the first time this ever happened to a young artist, but I couldn't break out of the prison of my own conceit. Its atmosphere slowly stifled not only my sense of humor but my sense of reality as well.

I had started out wanting to be a writer of suspense and adventure stories. Yes, I wanted my stories to be fresh and rich and original. Of course, I wanted them to be full of the stuff of life. I had seen this done in Hitchcock's movies and Chandler's novels and in supernatural thrillers like *Dracula* and *Frankenstein* and the stories of Edgar Allan Poe. It was not so far-fetched to think I had the ability to make good things in those traditions. But now, to say I began to see myself as a talent of Shakespearean genius would be to understate the grandeur of my delusions. I began to imagine my vision was prophetic, even salvific. I began to feel I might be born to utter things kept secret since the foundation of the world.

This thought closed over me bit by bit. It came to obsess me. Over the years, my writing became unreadable and un-publishable. Even Ellen, a ceaseless supporter of my ambitions, began to admit she could not always understand what I was trying to say. She did not know how deranged I was becoming, but she could see how unhappy I was.

The more my work was rejected, the more windy and insistent my ego became. If I was a failure always short of money it must be because the world did not understand me, and if the world did not understand me it was because my genius was too incomprehensibly great.

I don't remember when I first conceived the notion of writing a novel about Jesus Christ. I think the underlying motivation was this: if the public could not discover my unique brilliance in the subtleties of a lyrical mystery novel like *Face of the Earth*, then I would bludgeon them over the head with it by deconstructing the intricate psychological and cultural meanings lodged in the central figure of human history. That ought to do it.

Since my first reading of the Bible, I had continued to study Christianity from time to time and other religions as well. My interest was always cool and intellectual. I was not religious in any way and I was not drawn to faith. I called myself an agnostic at this point, but like most agnostics, I was a functional atheist.

I did think religion mattered, though. I thought of it as a living myth that shaped the human mind and expressed our innermost fears and desires. Many of the thinkers I knew and read dismissed the power of religion over people's lives. They thought faith was just a relic of mankind's superstitious past, something we were growing out of now in our scientific age.

I thought that was wrong. I agreed with the literary critic M. H. Abrams who wrote, "Secular thinkers have no more been able to work free of the centuries-old Judeo-Christian culture than Christian theologians were able to work free of their inheritance of classical and pagan thought."[1]

I thought that to be ignorant of Christianity was to be ignorant of the underpinnings of our own worldview. So when I began my research into mythology for *Face of the Earth*, I paid special attention to the gospel story. I saw it as the foundational myth of the West, the Great Narrative that had expressed and fashioned the Western mind-set more than any other.

Which was true enough, as far as it went. Christianity *is* the great Western narrative, whether you believe in it or not. And the idea of reinterpreting that narrative through fiction wasn't necessarily outlandish either. It had been done brilliantly and provocatively by Nikos Kazantzakis in his novel *The Last Temptation of Christ*, a book I admired very much.

In me, however, the scheme was simple madness. It was an act of narcissism, sorrow, and rage, at once grandiose and petty. Though Kazantzakis's novel was radical and shocked the religious authorities of his day, it was at least a serious exploration of Jesus as God incarnate, the savior of mankind. My book, on the other hand, simply sought to disassemble this Christ figure and explain his influence away. Fraser in his *Golden Bough* had shown us that Christianity was just one more death-and-resurrection cult among many. Freud in his *Totem and Taboo* and *Future of an Illusion* had shown us it was merely a projection of our father fixation on the heavens.

And now I—glorious, brilliant, postmodern I—would bring the source of that psychological mythology living to the page.

My Jesus would be the tortured vessel of our signifiers, the miserable expression of our existential angst. He would find enlightenment, yes, but it would be the enlightened acceptance of material existence, death, and suffering. In denial of this revelation, the mob would reject him, kill him, and then deify him as a way of silencing his existential truth. My Jesus would be myself, in other words—a rejected genius—and I would become he in the creation of him: the failed storyteller resurrected as the Greatest Storyteller of All Time.

It was still early in my self-education. I didn't really have the wherewithal to take on such a task, if anyone ever could. To my credit, I approached my work seriously. I holed myself away and read and researched and thought and wrote and outlined—which sent me crazier by the day. The failure of my first novel and the sudden shock of having pulled myself from a job I loved to lock myself up again in solitary study, threw me into horrible troughs of dissociation and melancholy. I would lose track of myself for half an hour at a time. I would come around to find myself in my car on some strange forest road without knowing where I was or how I had gotten there. I would have to find a gas station with a pay phone and call my wife so she could talk me through the process of getting home. For the first time, serious thoughts of suicide began to come to me. Nothing vivid or specific yet, just the notion: *a moment's suffering and then this pain would end.* But I went on working. What was madness, after all, but the burden of genius in a world of fools?

Ellen got a job with a small magazine in Boston. We moved there. I didn't care where I lived, or thought I didn't. We found an apartment in a house in Somerville, a working-class suburb that had been hit hard by the worsening recession. My money was almost gone and Ellen wasn't making much. Our apartment was large but we couldn't afford to furnish it so its rooms were all but empty. We had to put cardboard boxes in our secondhand refrigerator because we couldn't afford to buy shelves. We ate noodles for dinner almost every night, except when we splurged and went down to the corner for a fast-food hamburger. In the street beneath our windows, angry drunks, out of work, screamed at their wives and at each other. In the neighboring house, pressed close to ours, an old man coughed up the last of his smoke-riddled lungs.

Ellen's boss was a nasty tyrant and so her job made her increasingly unhappy. I found weekend work as a security guard in a bank, standing idle in uniform through empty hours, bored and depressed.

And during the week, day after day, at home alone while Ellen was at work, I sat tailor-fashion on the carpet of one of our unfurnished rooms, with books and notebooks spread out all around me. Gripping my fountain pen, I wrote for hours, feverishly. I once produced more than 150 handwritten pages in a single session. I kept the blinds drawn to block out the neighborhood. It drove our two cats insane and they fought each other viciously, climbing up the windows and slashing the blinds to ribbons while I worked on. In the afternoons, I would walk aimlessly around the city, dejected, daydreaming.

I would haunt Harvard Yard, yearning to be part of the college life I had always despised. I would wander into pinball parlors and feed precious quarters into the machines.

By the time the book was finished, I was an emotional cripple, barely able to think or speak or do anything but wander the city and dream. Was the completed work any good? I don't know anymore. I threw the manuscript away many years ago, so I can't go back and read it now and make an honest assessment of its qualities. I think I did as good a job at what I set out to do as I could. I can't really say any more than that.

I titled the book *Son of Man*. It took me weeks of backbreaking labor to type up its hundreds of handwritten pages. Then I sent the manuscript off to the famous editor in New York, now back from rehab. Weeks went by. No answer came. An agony of suspense. Finally the editor called. The book, he said, was a work of genius. Unique, explosively brilliant, revolutionary. But the subject matter was so controversial, he could not publish it without support from the other editors in the house. He didn't want a repeat of what had happened to *Face of the Earth*, orphaned at publication. He needed to get more readings.

Again, weeks passed. Waiting. Terrible. Then the devastating news. The other editors at the publishing house had universally rejected the novel. My editor sent me their letters. They ranged from the outraged to the dismissive.

My editor kindly helped me find a new agent for the manuscript, but the book never sold and I lost faith in it. Years later, I would write an extremely condensed version of the story and publish it with a small press, but I was just being stubborn at that point, refusing to take no for an answer. I worked hard at the new book, but I could not recover the inspiration of my madness. The version I published was hobbled and unformed. I'm sorry I did it.

Ellen and I decided to flee the scene of our unhappiness. We left Boston and rented a cottage on the edge of a forest preserve in the suburban New York county of Westchester. It was a beautiful miniature three-story house, built in the era of the Revolution. It was set in a secluded rural spot, only an hour out of the city. Ellen went back to work at the literary agency. I was able to pick up freelance assignments from my old newspaper and continue some well-paying secretarial work I'd begun doing for Harvard.

But if I had thought to come here to recover emotionally, it was a mistake. With no money, we couldn't afford cars that worked. Our otherwise elegant driveway was always littered with the shells of broken jalopies. Half the time I was stranded in the cottage and couldn't go anywhere. There was no Internet yet, no cell phones. I was stuck where I was, alone with myself. At another time, it might have been idyllic. I was surrounded by forest, which I'd always loved. I had time to read and write, to hike in the woods and fish in the reservoir at the bottom of the gorge. But I was furious and frustrated and confused by my failures and thwarted ambitions. The solitude turned me in on myself. I descended into painful and obsessive self-analysis to try to untie the tangle of my anguish. My writing became obscure and bizarre.

As my money dwindled, as my books and stories were rejected everywhere, my heart filled with paranoia and rage. It was agonizing. I saw saboteurs like my father all around me. I thought everyone—family, friends, colleagues—was out to hurt me, trip me up, betray me. They tried to hide their hostility—maybe they even hid it from themselves—but I saw the signs. They didn't want me to succeed, and it made me mad.

My wife seemed especially threatening to me, because I had trusted her and we were so intimately close. I was suspicious of everything she did now. Everything she did infuriated me. I remember once coming upon a bath towel Ellen had left lying on the bathroom floor. The sight of it filled me with fury. How thoughtless she was to just leave it there! What an insult to my manhood to be forced to pick up after her! It was obviously purposeful on her part. She wanted to belittle me and render me powerless. Well, I wasn't going to stand for it! I spent the day rehearsing the brutal things I was going to say to her when she got home. My hands fairly itched to get ahold of her . . .

Our marriage saved me here. I wanted so badly to say something cruel to Ellen, even to do something violent to her. But I loved her too much and she was too good to me. An intelligent and insightful woman, she had grown up with a writer father and knew what writers were like and what they needed. She was old-fashioned, feminine, tender, and generous—a dedicated homemaker who took careful care of me. The idea that she was plotting against me made no sense. The idea that she was working against me made no sense. Even I could see that, even then.

Because our marriage was what it was, because my wife was who she was, and because I loved her, my rage came to seem like a stranger to me. It felt to me like some red satanic hand trying to work me like a puppet. I fought it. When my wife came home, I swallowed all my fine, lacerating speeches. I told her what was happening inside me, carefully describing my crazy thought process step by step. As morose and brooding as I sometimes became, as angry as I sometimes felt, I never took it out on her, never even raised my voice to her. This fight was just between me and the devil of my rage.

But the madness had another side, equally tormenting. Something in me must have been horrified by the violence bubbling up in me. It set off an answering explosion of guilt and shame. My mind began to punish me with rampant hypochondria. It took me over entirely. I'd never experienced anything like it before. I would find a mark on my skin, an irregularity in my flesh, and I'd become certain it was cancer. I would lie awake each night in a cold sweat of fear. Each day, I would discover some new symptom that convinced me I was dying. After a while, I could barely think of anything else but the disease I knew I had. I would go to work and sit at my desk for hours without producing so much as a usable paragraph. Probing my own flesh. Fretting. Afraid.

What a wreck I was! Rage, guilt, terror. My heart was hell. The pain was so intense, I abandoned my agnosticism for an eccentric, puling spirituality. I prayed wildly for help to a god I didn't believe in. I grew mystic and weird. I would try to mentally cast myself out of myself, to project my soul into a tree or a stone in order to separate myself from my own pain. Sometimes, amazingly enough, it actually worked. My mind would seem to travel elsewhere. The agony of anger and fear would subside. For a few minutes. A few hours maybe. Then it all came back: rage, guilt, terror. What a wreck.

The strangest part of all this was that I didn't realize how abnormal it was. My psyche was crumbling like a ruined tower in some gothic romance and I thought it was just the way things were. After all, I had always had periods of depression and mental difficulty. The Bola—it was just part of me. Wasn't that the way things were for any honest-thinking man in this existential horror show of a world? To think is to suffer, isn't it? To think is to know the nearness of death, to understand the ambivalence of love, to carry the weight of tragedy on your shoulders. Isn't it? Isn't that what it means to be an artist and intellectual?

I didn't know that this was madness. I thought that it was life.

So in the midst of this lunacy, I just trudged on. I worked every day. I went on reading through my stacks of books. My bank account dwindled, but I always managed to avoid absolute zero with some freelance gig or other. My wife and I wanted children, so we simply went ahead with our plans and Ellen got pregnant. That only made our situation more impossible, of course. We both wanted Ellen to be an at-home mother, and my income was nowhere near enough to support us in that.

At one point, it actually occurred to me that—hey, since I'd always wanted to write suspense stories—maybe I ought to dash one off. I would do it under a pseudonym, of course. It wasn't part of my real work of salvific revelation. It was just a way to make some money. I plotted out the novel carefully then enlisted one of my younger brothers, Laurence, a talented playwright, to help me. He and I pounded out the first hundred pages in three days. We not only sold it—the first check arrived as my bank balance dropped to mere pennies—we won the Edgar Award for best paperback mystery and got a movie deal as well. In my heart of hearts, I knew that telling such stories was my gift. I was just too magnificent to stoop to using it.

I don't know how long I would have gone on like this. I've seen people waste their whole lives mired in this kind of psychic trouble. This is just the way I am, they think. This is just the way life is. Maybe I got lucky, or maybe my wild, mystic, lunatic prayers were heard. But finally something happened that, quite literally, opened my eyes to the truth of my situation.

One day during this period, I went fishing at a local reservoir with a friend. He and I went out on a rowboat together and worked the water through dawn into early morning. My friend was a Texas-bred yarn-spinner. As we sat in the boat, he began to tell me a long story about an airplane mechanic. The mechanic, he said, had been lying on his back under a plane's wing working with a screwdriver. The mechanic got distracted—I don't remember how—and the tool slipped from his fingers. It fell on him point downward and poked out his eye. Naturally, the story made a deep impression on my delicate hypochondriacal nerves.

A few weeks later, I was assembling a new writing desk in

my attic workspace. Ellen was sitting in my swivel chair, chatting with me to keep me company. I was lying on my back under the desk, tightening up the drawer slide with a screwdriver. The phone rang and I crawled out from under the desk to answer it.

A familiar voice on the other end of the line brought me disturbing news. One of my brothers had had an emotional breakdown. There had been a dramatic scene. The crisis had passed. He was seeing a psychiatrist. All would be well.

I said the appropriate words and hung up the phone. I told my wife what had happened. We both felt sorrow for my brother, but we assured each other everything would be all right. I climbed back under the desk, lay on my back again, and went on tightening the drawer slide with my screwdriver.

But in a few more moments, my hand began to shake. My fingers went weak. The screwdriver slipped from my grasp and fell toward my face, point down. It struck me just beneath the orbit of the eye, right on the hard edge at the top of the cheekbone. Then it tumbled harmlessly to the floor.

With that, realization opened in me like a flower. I suddenly saw how broken I was. All this time, despite the arguments with my father, despite his unkindness to me and my anger at him, despite my mother's disengagement and distance, despite the violence and anxiety of my school days, despite my long retreat into fantasy, I had tried to tell myself I had had a happy childhood in a happy family. I had tried to tell myself my suffering was just a normal part of a thinking man's life. I had tried to tell myself that my inability to sell my unreadable work was the world's fault.

My brother's pain dispelled all those illusions in a moment. In him, I saw myself, and I realized I was wrong. It was all wrong. My childhood had been miserable. My upbringing had been twisted and hostile. My view of myself was delusional. My view of reality was completely unreal. This wasn't life. This wasn't ordinary life at all. Something was wrong inside me. Something was terribly wrong.

I recovered the screwdriver. I slowly climbed out from under the desk. I tossed the tool down on the desktop, my hand still shaking. I looked at my wife.

"It's not just my brother," I said. "It's me too. I need help."

CHAPTER 11

FIVE EPIPHANIES

I have lived two lives. That was the ending of the first: that screwdriver falling. Within days, I had made an appointment with a psychiatrist in Manhattan. What followed was a miracle of recovery, a swift, dramatic, and absolute transformation from one way of being to another. I sometimes like to joke that I've seen many men go mad, but I'm the only person I've ever met who has gone sane. It's not really a joke, though. Sigmund Freud is often quoted describing the psycho-therapeutic process as a journey from "hysterical misery to ordinary unhappiness." My journey was different: it was a passage from suicidal despair to a fullness of vitality and joy I had not even thought to imagine.

While now I look back on this period and see Christ within it everywhere, at the time, on the surface, he was apparent only in hints and whispers. This was—or seemed—an entirely secular conversion. But it was this conversion that made my ultimate conversion to Christianity possible, and maybe inevitable, because it freed me to trust my own perceptions and reasoning. As long as I was in mental disarray, as long as my actions were self-destructive, as long as my outlook was deluded, any faith I thought to have, any idea of God I formed, seemed to me by definition unreliable, the comforting illusion of a mind in pain. As long as religion might even appear to serve me as an emotional crutch, I dismissed it as a form of weakness. It was only when I felt certain that my inner life was healthy and my understanding was sound that I could begin to accept what experience and logic had been leading me to believe. For others, I know it was Christ who led them to joy. For me, it was joy that led me to Christ.

These crossroad years, these five years of therapy, were emotionally dramatic. They were full of sudden and consequential insights, unexpected thunderclaps of comprehension that permanently changed the way I thought and lived. There were so many of them, I'm almost afraid to set them down here all together. I'm afraid I'll come across as even loopier than I was, some sort of flighty mystic leaping from inspiration to inspiration like a celestial ballet dancer leaping from cloud to cloud. It wasn't like that, though. I was just a writer making his way, a little slowed by personal damage, a little late to the game. But a writer, to find his voice, must first find himself. I found myself in an electric season of growth and transition, and the discovery was marked by this rapid series of revelations.

I'm going to make a catalogue of those epiphanies here, because they were not only the souvenirs of my journey to sanity, they were the prized relics I carried with me into a better time. I referred back to them continually in the years that followed. I studied them carefully. They became the basis for the way I thought and for the things I thought. Ultimately, I came to believe they were not so much a series of revelations as fragments of a single revelation, spread out along the five-year path. In effect, I would spend the next decade learning to put those fragments together in their proper arrangement. Only then did I see the meaning of the greater epiphany complete.

—⊶—

A year or two after I entered therapy, I found myself sitting alone at my desk in the late hours of a spring night. I was trying to decide whether or not to end my life. It was the last time I would ever think of killing myself, but it was the worst time; the darkest. I had never considered the idea quite so seriously before.

My wife and I had moved back to Manhattan. We had a baby daughter, Faith. I had a low-level job at a movie studio: not much money, but a steady paycheck with benefits and a flexible schedule that left me plenty of time to write. Ellen and I were both taking freelance work, too, so we were getting by. We had a pleasant one-bedroom apartment in midtown. The neighborhood was good and the rent was low. But it was a small place for a family of three. We had to wall off a dining alcove as a nursery. And our bedroom had to serve double duty as my office, which frequently discommoded my ever-patient and supportive wife.

I was locked away in the office-bedroom that miserable midnight. I was sitting at the same desk I'd been building when I dropped the screwdriver a year and a half before. I had gone in there to work, as I usually did in the evenings, but my work was over now. The baby was in her crib and Ellen was asleep on the living room sofa. I had poured myself a drink—I kept a bottle in the desk drawer like the private eyes did in my favorite novels. I had turned off every light except a desk lamp. I had the radio on, tuned to a baseball game, the volume low. I was just sitting there in the dark, staring into the shadows, smoking cigarette after cigarette, taking an occasional sip of scotch.

I felt a brutal weight of sorrow in me—sorrow and self-pity, a toxic blend. I was a burden to my family, I thought. I thought: *My wife and daughter would be better off without me.* I don't know now how serious I was. Serious enough. I was reviewing the various methods by which I might end it all. Walking off the roof of the building seemed the easiest way. I was pretty sure I had the courage for it. I was even beginning to make plans for when I might do it.

One sentence kept repeating itself in my mind, one refrain: *I don't know how to live. I don't know how to live . . .*

Most suicidal people don't do the deed when their mood is lowest. They're too depressed. They don't have the energy to act so decisively. It's when they start to feel better—that's when the real danger arises. And I had been feeling better this last year or so, much better off and on. But the therapy that was helping me was painful too. I could only afford to see my psychiatrist once a week, but the process was on my mind every day, every hour, and the obsessive self-exploration was exposing parts of my past and my psyche I would have much rather left hidden away. Plus I still had no real idea of how to get along in the world, how to achieve the things I wanted, the career I wanted, the good life I wanted for my wife and child. I could not find a way to use my particular talents as a writer to convey the vision I wanted to convey. My writing career, such as it had ever been, had ground to a complete halt. I hadn't had a serious publication in almost five years.

Then, earlier that day, there'd been a bitter little incident; just a small thing, but cruelly calibrated to unbalance me. I was walking across town, downhearted, lost in my own melancholy reverie, when I glanced up and spotted the famous editor who had published my first novel. He was on the same sidewalk as I was, coming right toward me. Jarred out of my meditations, I wasn't quick enough to realize that he had already seen me and was trying to walk past with his eyes averted, trying to avoid a meeting. Reflexively, I called out hello. He stopped, but only for a second. He was brusque and dismissive, even disdainful. Stone-faced, he said a word or two, then quickly walked on. Like every other editor on the planet, he wanted nothing to do with me. It was a little thing, as I say. But I was already fragile with depression and it broke my heart.

So I came home at the end of the day. I dutifully finished my work. I sat there at my desk with my cigarettes and my scotch, my ballgame and my shadows and my sorrow. I sank into the depths of my anguish and I despaired.

What I didn't know, what I couldn't see, was that it was almost over: this difficult time; I was almost through it. I was already past the most painful phase of my therapy. I would soon experience a series of remarkable breakthroughs. My depression would lift for good, and the past would begin to lose its insidious grip on me. At that black, black moment, I was inches away, just inches away, from finding a light of true peace and gladness within myself.

Within weeks, the first hint of a change in my professional fortunes would make its way to me too. I would win a small poetry prize—a hundred dollars and publication— for a long poem I had distilled, ironically enough, from the transfiguration scene in my disastrous Jesus novel. Again, not a big deal, but a legitimate sign that I was finally starting to find my voice, finally starting to figure out how to say what I wanted to say in a way people could understand. Very soon after that, I would read a novel that would complete that process, changing the trajectory of my work and restoring me to my original purposes. *The Woman in White* by Wilkie Collins is a Victorian thriller so brilliant that some scholars suspect it was heavily rewritten by Collins's good friend and publisher Charles Dickens. Two-thirds of the way through reading the book, I would literally sit up in bed with the shock of understanding. I would suddenly see, like looking through a clock to the clockwork, the mechanics of how the thrilling stories I loved to write could convey whatever vision of the world I had. The moment would mark the beginning of my career; it would be the making of it.

It was all right there, a good life, a joyful life, the life I hungered for, so close to me, a footstep in time, as I sat there at my desk and considered suicide, thinking the same words over and over again: *I don't know how to live.*

The baseball game on the radio was a Mets game. I'd been a Yankees fan all my life, but the Yanks were in the doldrums this year and the Mets had assembled an exciting roster of players. I'd become fascinated by them. I identified with them, especially with the two veterans who led the team. They were a mismatched pair. Their contrary personalities seemed to represent something of importance to me. One, Keith Hernandez, the first baseman, was a dark, brooding, cigarette-smoking man-on-the-town type, a student of Civil War history, and a Gold Glove student of the game. Away from the stadium, he was involved in a divorce and a drug scandal. But I loved the thinking man's way he had reinvented the defensive work of the infield. When I began to experiment with my first crime novels after reading *The Woman in White*, I would use the name Keith as part of my pseudonym.

The other player, the catcher Gary Carter, was Hernandez's opposite, a sunny, upbeat, gung-ho future Hall-of-Famer who never stopped grinning and liked to refer to himself as "the Kid." Carter was a clean-living Christian, and a loud-mouth about it. During postgame interviews, he would frequently thank the Lord Jesus for a victory or a home run. He once said that he could see the interviewer's smile curdle whenever he did it. I could see it, too, and, in all honesty, I always sympathized with the interviewer. I considered Carter's exuberant faith a character flaw. It embarrassed me. To paraphrase the cynical hero of one of my own novels: Whenever I heard some-one say *Jesus* as if he really meant it, it made my skin crawl, as if they'd said *squid* or *intestine* instead. The rest of the Mets, a talented assembly of scoundrels and troublemakers, openly hated the Kid for his relentlessly clean-cut cheer. But I liked the guy. His all-out play inspired me.

Now, as I sat at my desk in a cloud of smoke and self-pitying sadness, the announcer on the radio described Carter stepping up to bat. It was a crucial moment in a close game. There were men on base in scoring position. Carter smacked a grounder to the outfield. A notoriously slow runner because of his bad knees, he took off down the line as fast as he could. Somehow he managed to beat the throw to first. The single scored the winning runs. It was an exciting moment, but I was barely listening. I hardly cared. I just went on thinking: *I don't know how to live. I don't know how to live.*

When the game was over, the on-field reporter corralled Carter for a postvictory interview. The reporter asked how the catcher was able to run so fast when his knees were so badly damaged from years of squatting behind home plate. If, in that moment, Carter had done his Jesus routine, if he had praised Christ or sung hallelujah, I don't think his com-ments would have reached me at all. I think I would have grimaced and shuddered at his happy-talk piety. Then I would have shrugged it off and gone on toying with the notion of self-murder.

But tonight, for some reason—for some reason—Carter

decided to leave the religious stuff out of it. Instead, he answered very simply. He said, "Sometimes you just have to play in pain."

The words jarred me instantly out of my depressive reverie. I remember blinking in the shadows as if waking up. I remember slowly turning my gaze from the empty darkness to the radio. I remember repeating the sentence silently to myself. It seemed to me for all the world as if Carter had heard my thoughts as I sat there. It seemed to me he had heard me thinking, *I don't know how to live*, and had responded over the airwaves with the only honest answer there is.

Sometimes you just have to play in pain.

I nodded in the darkness, my eyes growing damp. I thought: *Yes. That's right. That's it exactly. And I can do that too. I can play in pain. If I have to. I know I can. That's something I actually know how to do.*

I put out my cigarette. I got out of my chair. I turned off the radio. I left the bedroom. I never considered suicide again.

⸎

From the very first day I started it, therapy had changed the rules of life for me. Up until then, I considered some of my most self-destructive and disturbing habits of mind to be inborn aspects of my nature. If I was unhappy, I thought it was just the way things were, the world being what it was, and me being who I was. Like a lot of artists, too, I assumed my suffering and whatever talent I had were inseparable. I was afraid that if I lost one, I would also sacrifice the other.

But as soon as my therapy began, I realized, no, none of this was true. My misery was not me and it was not the world and it was not connected to my talent, such as it was. It was just a wound I had sustained in the course of living, a wound that could be healed. It was a broken piece of the psychic machinery, and it could be fixed.

I've often wondered what that initial meeting was like for the psychiatrist because for me now it seems poignantly comical. Frantic with hypochondria, pale with depression, edgy with anger, I all but stumbled into his office that day. It was a cramped, windowless room on the ground floor of an ornate apartment building on Manhattan's west side. I dropped into the armchair and he sat in a high-backed swivel chair a few feet away from me. There was a Freudian couch against the wall to my right, a desk to my left, and hardly any space for anything else.

The psychiatrist was a slumped, sad-eyed Jewish man about ten or fifteen years older than me. He had a thin, quiet voice and spoke deliberately as if to make sure every word he chose was just the right one. He had a dry sense of humor, too, and I could tell right away he was smart, which mattered to me very much at the time. How could I expect a mere mortal to heal me if he couldn't comprehend my towering genius?

He asked how he could help me. In answer, I began talking and talking and talking some more. Over the next forty-five minutes or so, I believe I told him every single untoward, sad, and twisted thing I knew about myself. Bizarre sexual fantasies, homicidal hostilities, deviant desires, and antisocial behaviors, all of it. I had been thinking it over for years, you see. Probing my troubles, investigating their psychic causes. I knew the theories of Freud well, and I knew myself pretty well. Now everything I knew and thought I knew came pouring out of me in a torrent of words. I told all my darkest secrets in that first session with so much *brio* and abandon that the psychiatrist finally shifted in his seat and shook his head in puzzlement and said in his deliberate way, "Why are you telling me this?"

To which I replied, startled, "I thought you might need to know!"

When the fifty-minute hour ended, I left the little room. I left the ornate apartment building. Made my way back to work on the east side. I walked across Central Park. It was clean and green in the early autumn sunlight. I felt relieved to have that first session over with. I even felt slightly hopeful about the future. Other than that, though, I felt no different than I had before. I had told this doctor things on first meeting him— many things—that I had never told anyone ever. You would have thought making such a complete confession would have had some profound emotional effect on me. It didn't seem to. The world and I seemed about the same as ever. I shrugged to myself and continued on my way.

The next day at home—we still lived in the Westchester cottage then—I had to make a phone call to arrange an appointment. The phone was on a shelf off the narrow stairway that connected the ground-floor kitchen with the living room on the second floor. I sat on the stairs as I made my call. I remember I got into some minor squabble with a nasty receptionist and ended up slamming the handset down into its cradle with frustration.

Then, without any warning, I buried my face in my hands and began to weep.

I had not cried for years and years and I had not sobbed like this since childhood. My chest throbbed painfully with the force of the convulsions. My whole body shook and it went on and on. I understood. It was a delayed reaction to my first therapy session. I had shoveled three decades of muck out of my consciousness. Now my body was washing the vessel clean. I relaxed and let the process run its course.

The effect of the catharsis was remarkable. When it was over, it seemed as if every symptom of mental sickness had vanished from me for good and all. The anger, the depression, the hypochondria—as if by magic, they were all gone. For days and days afterward, I felt a radiance of light and life rising inside me, a kind of inner dawn. I felt at once still and hilarious, and I knew this was my True and Original Self reborn. My interior cosmos wheeled in harmony with the stars, and the little birds of happiness sang tweet, tweet, tweet . . . and yes, all right, I knew it was temporary. I didn't think I'd been cured of my lifelong mental affliction in one fifty-minute session. I knew all the old agonies would soon come clamoring back to their home in my brain.

Still, while it lasted, it was a glorious sensation. More than that. I believed that these few days of high peace gave me a momentary glimpse of something true. This, I thought, was who I really was, not that other miserable man I had been living with all these years. This inner harmony was the goal toward which I would be working in my therapy. And it was real. It existed. I was experiencing it right now, like a vision of things to come. There was a long trek of self-understanding ahead of me, I knew. But for those few days, I was allowed to visit the promised land on the other side.

For years, maybe most of my life, I had languished in that typical young intellectual's delusion that gloom and despair are the romantic lot of the brilliant and the wise. But now I saw: it wasn't so. Why should it be? What sort of wisdom has no joy in it? What good is wisdom without joy? By joy I don't mean ceaseless happiness, of course. I don't mean willed stupidity for the sake of a cheap smile. The world is sad and it is suffering. A tragic sense is essential to both realism and compassion. By joy I mean a vital love of life in both sorrow and gladness. Why not? The hungry can't eat your tears. The poor can't spend them. They're no comfort to the afflicted and they don't bring the wicked to justice. Everything useful that can be done in the world can be done in joy.

For the first time in what seemed forever, I began to believe that I might make my way back to the man I was meant to be.

———∞———

The next shock of revelation came only four months later. This one was the most spectacular: the one truly mystical experience I have ever had in my life.

It was December now. My wife had entered the final days of her pregnancy. This was during the first popularity of so-called "natural childbirth," in which the woman used no painkilling drugs or procedures but endured labor with only breathing techniques and massages to alleviate her suffering. Our obstetrician, a squat, gruff, no-nonsense Italian American woman, responded to the fad sarcastically. "Since when did nature become our friend?" she asked. It was a good question. But we were caught up in the fashion and devoted to the idea.

The truth was, the most positive aspect of "natural childbirth" was probably the least "natural," the least primitive; a genuine innovation. In "natural childbirth," husbands relinquished their traditional role of pacing and chain-smoking cigarettes in the hospital hallway during the labor. Adam had probably done something like this during the birth of Cain and Abel, but no more. Instead, in "natural childbirth," the father served as a "birth coach," attending his wife in the delivery room. This enabled him to lend her some moral support for what that was worth. But more important—or at least more dramatic—was the fact, it allowed him to witness the birth of his child.

Ellen and I dutifully attended a seemingly endless series of classes during which we practiced the natural childbirth breathing and massage techniques. Even a mere male like myself could see these would be more or less useless against the agonies of labor, but I showed up and did my part. It was during these classes that I noticed I had a powerful emotional reaction to the instructional films that showed real births. The precise instant when the baby slid from its mother into the world always affected me deeply. Every time I saw it, I found it poignant and awesome.

Our teachers instructed us to make a pregnancy kit, a small gym bag full of the tools the birth coach would use to help his wife through her travail. I don't remember now what this seemingly random collection of objects was (it included tennis balls for some reason) but the bag developed a totemic significance for us. It became an emblem of the comforts of the "natural" approach. On the night my wife went into labor, I calmly escorted her down the narrow cottage steps and picked up the pregnancy bag waiting by the kitchen door. We walked out into the driveway where I calmly rested the bag on the car's roof and helped my wife into the passenger seat. I then calmly went around to the driver's side, slid in behind the wheel, and calmly drove away, calmly forgetting the bag so that it tumbled from the car roof to the gravel, not to be seen again until our return home some days later.

We reached the hospital in the city and checked in. There followed thirteen hours of brutal labor with no drugs, no spinal blocks, and not even any tennis balls. My wife is the gentlest and most feminine of women, but she has, I swear, a core of iron. Nothing but my absolute insistence would have deterred her from seeing this through to the finish drug free. And while even at twenty-eight I liked to think of myself as a patriarchal tyrant, I tended to limit my absolute insistence to calling for a cocktail before dinner. In more important matters, I trusted Ellen's judgment and wanted only her happiness.

So, through the night and on into a snowy morning, she was tortured on the rack of her contractions. The only comic relief came from a pretty little blond nurse who took a liking to me—I was a handsome devil then!—and kept running into the room to rub my shoulders in order to help me bear my wife's pain. Ellen's reaction to this was unprintable in a book about religion but, trust me, it was hilarious.

Sometime during the last hours of the labor, Ellen discharged some meconium—fetal stool. In our classes, we had been taught that this was a sign the baby might be in some sort of trouble. "Fetal distress" was the nice phrase for it. My wife's eyes were already glazed with pain and exhaustion, but now I saw the hot-white light of panic come into them. We pressed the alarm button by the bed to call for help. A new nurse hurried in, a serious-looking brunette in her late twenties, as I was. It was strange, but the moment she walked through the door I straightened and she stopped in her tracks and we realized that we knew each other. Ellen and I told her about the meconium. The nurse took one look at Ellen and saw her up-spiraling terror. She sat on the bed and held my wife by the shoulders, peered deep into her eyes, and said forcefully, "This baby is fine." Ellen believed her and her panic faded away.

The nurse's name was Ann Christiano. No, it really was. From then on, she tended to us with warmth and kindness and expert skill. She and I tried to figure out where we'd met before, but we couldn't. In fact, after talking it over, we decided it was unlikely we had ever laid eyes on each other, but the feeling that we were old acquaintances persisted nonetheless. The last time Ellen and I saw her was after the baby came. Mother, father, and child were huddled together, spent, on the narrow hospital bed. Ann Christiano crept in quietly. She raised the bedrail to keep us from tumbling out. She put a blanket over us, all three, and tucked us in—and left us forever. Ellen and I solemnly agreed that, given her name, she must have been an angel sent to us in our hour of need.

When at last our daughter was ready to be born, here is what happened.

I had not been sure what my reaction would be to the gore and mess of childbirth. Some men faint dead away, I've heard, while some don't mind it. I had no way of knowing how I would feel or behave. Birth is a dramatically material business. Great gouts of blood and urine and feces come out of the mother in gushes and floods. From the perspective of a watching husband, it is a deluge that purges your wife of every trace of ladylike delicacy and feminine mystery. This is the woman you love, remember, whose body is erotic to you and alluring in just those places that are now so violently soiled. It's bound to make an impact on a man's mind one way or another, and it would be completely understandable if he were shocked or disgusted or repelled. I wasn't, though. I hadn't known this up to that moment, but it turned out I had the same attitude toward human gore as I'd always had to human depravity: just because it's usually hidden doesn't mean it isn't always there. When it did become visible, it struck me as a normal thing and I felt no need to look away.

In fact, after a while, as the process went on, I began to formulate a strange idea about it. It began to seem to me that the aggressive, convulsive physicality of this experience was uniting my wife and me in a new level of intimacy. Through the blood and guts of birth, we were being carried into a togetherness that was almost super-temporal: above time, beyond time. Until now, whenever I had read that passage in Genesis about a husband and wife becoming "one flesh," I had thought it referred to sex. But no—no, that was fanciful, I thought now, a romantic fiction. The old sages had known much better than that. The unity of sex, which was the beginning of this labor and the cause of it, was also just a symbol of a greater unifying power. Even the child herself, this child being born, the one flesh of marriage literally personified, was only a symbol.

Sex, birth, marriage, these bodies, this life, they were all just representations of the power that had created them, the power now surging through my wife in this flood of matter, the power that had made us one: the power of love. Love, I saw now, was an exterior spiritual force that swept through our bodies in the symbolic forms of eros, then bound us materially, skin and bone, in the symbolic moment of birth. Everything we were, everything we were going through—it was all merely living metaphor. Only the love was real.

What happened next, then, was not a vision or an hallucination. It was a spiritual event. I saw it. I felt it. I experienced it, as surely as you would experience a kiss on the lips or a punch in the nose. I have never been through anything else like it. It was as real as it was impossible.

The baby came—that moment came that moved me so deeply whenever I saw it even on film—and the surging torrent of creation swept me away. The borders of my self shattered like a barrier of glass and out I flowed. My consciousness, my psyche, the whole invisible presence of me was carried out of my body on the tide of love. I became not one flesh with my wife but one being beyond flesh with the love I felt for her. My spirit washed into that love and became part of it, a splash in a rushing river. In that river of love, I went raging down the plane of Ellen's body until the love I was and the love that carried me melded with the love I felt for the new baby we had made together and I became part of that love as well and then . . .

Then, like living water rushing at full speed into the open sea, I saw I was about to flow out into the infinite. I saw that, beyond the painted scenery of mere existence, it was all love, love unbounded, mushrooming, vast, alive, and everlasting. The love I felt, the love I was, was about to cascade into the very origin of itself, the origin of our three lives and of all creation.

This experience was over in half a second. Not a full second; only half. In a reflex of fear, I drew myself back into myself before I could be carried entirely away. I regretted that reflex immediately. Why had I stopped the process? What might I have seen, where would I have gotten to, had I just let it go? Would I have fainted? Died? Would I have touched the gates of heaven? The face of God? If nothing else, a writer's curiosity should have compelled me to follow the event to its conclusion. As a reporter, I had once dashed into a burning house just to see what it looked like inside. Couldn't I have let my ego flow into the underlying truth of reality just to see what *it* looked like inside?

Well, never mind. Here was the baby, ten fingers and ten toes. And here was the happy mother, glowing and triumphant. The visionary moment was over.

But what had happened had happened. I had seen what I had seen. For years, I would try to rationalize it away but I never quite could. I was there. I went through it. Me, my spirit—in the flood of creation, at the delta of the sea of love.

I would never forget it.

—⦿—

After that, I began to haunt churches. Not often, but sometimes. I'd duck into some fine old landmark on my way from one Manhattan location to another. I'd sit in a pew in the shadows. I'd contemplate the icons and the stations of the cross or simply gaze up into the high, vaulted spaces and occasionally launch a prayer just to see what would happen. This was different from the sweaty, desperate, cowardly religiosity that had overtaken me during the worst of my depression and hypochondria. These church visits were spontaneous, contemplative, tentative, and calm.

I had seen something when my daughter was born and I did not know what to make of it. My postmodern skepticism had been shaken and yet . . . I was still at the beginning of therapy. I was just emerging from the haze of craziness and delusion. I did not trust myself. I did not trust that I had seen what I saw. "Why do you doubt your senses?" the ghost of Jacob Marley asks Ebenezer Scrooge. "Because," Scrooge replies, "a little thing affects them." Maybe my vision in the delivery room was just a trick of the brain. A release of chemicals under stress.

But such explanations couldn't entirely silence the voice of the revelation. It raised serious questions about how I was living, what I was doing, and what was happening to me. Here I was in a course of psychotherapy more or less based on the theories of Freud. Therapy was already helping me so much that the work of Freud was becoming like scripture to me. His worldview was beginning to seem to me unassailable. But Freud, in effect, had declared that all spiritual things were merely symbols of the flesh. In the delivery room, for the first time, it had seemed to me that he had gotten it exactly the wrong way round. Our flesh was the symbol. It was the love that was real.

Why, after all, should the flesh be the ground floor of our interpretations? Why should we end our understanding at the level of material things? It's just a prejudice really. The flesh is convincing. We can see it, feel it, smell it, taste it. It's very there. It's a trick of the human mind to give such presence the weight of reality. Men kill each other over dollar bills that are only paper because the paper has come to seem more real to them than the time and value it represents. In the same way, and for the same reason, people destroy themselves and everyone around them for sex: because sex has come to seem more real to them than the love it was made to express.

I had seen that love, seen it with my own eyes. And if that vision was just a release of chemicals, well, so was my vision of the trees and the sidewalks and the whole city. I saw it all through the mechanics and chemistry and electricity of the brain and yet it was still, in some true sense, there. I could head east from Fifth Avenue and reliably reach Madison, turn south from 53rd and get to 52nd every single time. The scientist—or the Buddhist—might declare such perceptions were illusions, but not one of them would head uptown to get to the Bowery. They knew what they knew. They saw what they saw.

So did I. I had seen beyond the scrim of the physical world and it was all love, living love, a love of which our human love, our human lives, were only a manifestation and a symbol. I did not know what to make of it.

Somewhere around this time, I met Doug Ousley, the rector of the landmark Episcopal Church of the Incarnation around the corner from my apartment, the priest who would one day baptize me. His wife had been playing with her babies on the rectory balcony and noticed my wife playing with her baby in the garden down below. The two mothers became acquainted. After Ellen gave Mary a copy of my transfiguration poem, we all got together.

The Ousleys were a comically mismatched couple: she delightfully vivacious, he phlegmatic, taciturn, and mordant. Doug was a dedicated pastor who spent a lot of his time sitting beside sickbeds and tending to his parishioners in their emergency needs. But I sometimes used to tease him that he was the worst priest ever, because he was gruff and sardonic and had none of the stagey warmth or bonhomie many pastors cultivate. In short, he was my kind of guy, and we became close friends.

It was good and helpful to talk religion with him as I tried to reason things through. He was widely read and carefully reasonable and he never preached at me. Sometimes I even attended services at Incarnation to hear his sermons and to enjoy the Bach cantatas sung by his excellent choir, which included Mary, a former professional singer. But really, it was the capacity for love behind his brusque exterior that gave his faith substance for me: specifically his love for his wife over the increasingly terrible years.

I was walking in our neighborhood one day and met Mary on the sidewalk outside the post office. I gave her a friendly hello and without prologue she fell sobbing into my arms. As I stood nonplussed and uncomprehending, she told me her foot had gone numb. I patted her back—there, there—and said it was probably nothing. It was not nothing. It was an early symptom of multiple sclerosis. Over the next twenty-five years, the disease killed that vital and affectionate woman by unbearable inches. And Doug never wavered in his devotion to her, never faltered in his love. It was a tough-guy performance for the ages, and he would not have been able to do it had he not been steeled by faith in Christ. It was a living sermon, his best.

The thing was, in my shiny new state of burgeoning sanity,

and in the aftermath of my vision in the delivery room, I was beginning to realize there was a spiritual side to life, a side I had been neglecting in my postmodern mind-set. Strip that spirituality away and you were left with a kind of "realism" that no longer seemed to me very realistic at all.

The spirit did not have to be supernatural. I thought of spirit simply as the pure internal human experience of life. This was the stuff my favorite poet John Keats wrote about: the full mingling of human consciousness with the song of a nightingale, say, or with the frieze on a Grecian urn. In Keats's greatest poem, "Ode to Autumn," that mingling becomes complete. The poet becomes one with the season of fruitfulness and death until it has a music as lovely as the songs of spring. In Keats's poems, the true fullness of reality does not take place outside of human consciousness but in conjunction with it so that

> "Beauty is truth, truth beauty"—that is all
> Ye know on earth, and all ye need to know.[1]

If we don't accept our inner experience as real, then only man's material desires have any meaning. Our yearnings for pleasure and power are all that's left. Anything else, anything that seems like absolute spiritual truth or absolute spiritual morality, must only be an elaborate illusion that can be deconstructed back down to those brute facts. This was Nietzsche's vision, the vision that Dostoevsky opposed in *Crime and Punishment* even before Nietzsche had written it down. And it was the vision of postmodernism now, too, the source of the postmodernist mission to endlessly analyze our spiritual experiences of truth and beauty in order to get to the materialist "reality" underneath.

It's a flattering philosophy for intellectuals, no doubt. Endless analysis is what they're good at. But the reductiveness and meaninglessness of the enterprise are creations of the enterprise itself. That is, you have to first make the assumption that material is the only reality before you can begin to reason away the spirit.

One night, walking along 8th Street in the East Village, I saw some adolescent boys, out too late and unattended. They were playing an arcade video game set up on the sidewalk, piloting a digital spacecraft through starlit infinity, blasting everything in their path to bits. Now and then, the machine would let out a robotic shout of encouragement: *You're doing great!* So the urchins flew on through the make-believe nothingness, destroying whatever they saw, hypnotized by the mechanical praise that stood in for the human voice of love. That, it seemed to me, was postmodernism in a nutshell. It ignored the full spiritual reality of life all around it in order to blow things apart inside a man-made box that only looked like infinity. *You're doing great, intellectuals! You're doing great.*

Much as Freudian-style therapy was helping me, I wanted something more. My research into Christianity had given me a lot of respect for its tragic vision of love. In the Bible, and in the minds of great theologians, Christ represented Love Despised, Love Rejected, Love Crucified in the world. That was a love I could believe in. It was in keeping with the things

I saw around me. But it was a love that was ultimately triumphant in the miracle of the resurrection and in the hope of faith. And I did not have faith, and I did not believe in miracles. Church doctrines seemed absurd to me. Born of a virgin. Resurrected from the grave. Coming in glory to judge the living and the dead. I could not buy into any of it.

To get around that roadblock, I tried the nondoctrinal Universalist church for a while—the "Church of Amorphous Rambling," in which I'd been married. But the church experience itself was alienating to my contrarian artist's soul. The ferociously radical-to-the-death Jesus of the Gospels was transformed here into a bland cheerleader for socially acceptable niceness. That made no sense to me. No one ever got himself crucified for organizing a charity golf tournament. As one friend, a lapsed believer, said to me of the church experience, "The services are pretty. It's the tuna casserole of it all I can't stand."

I couldn't stand the tuna casseroles either. I stopped going to church.

Instead, I came to zen and, through zen, I had my next epiphany—or *satori*, as the zen folks call it. The word is sometimes translated as *sudden enlightenment* or *awakening*, but my old friend Jack Kerouac wonderfully rendered it "a kick in the eye." That's what it was for me.

Zen, by definition, is impossible to define. The path that

can be spoken of is not the true path, and all that. The legend goes that the practice even began in silence, with the Buddha's famous Flower Sermon. Siddhartha held up a white lotus to his followers and said . . . absolutely nothing. No one understood him, except one disciple, who smiled. And with that smile, zen began.

It's really more a practice than a philosophy. Basically, you sit cross-legged and focus on nothing but your breath. This is called *zazen*, seated meditation. Sometimes as you sit, you count your breaths as an aid to concentration. Sometimes you focus on a *koan*, a sort of riddle that serves as a spur to enlightenment. *What is the sound of one hand clapping? What was your original face before you were born?* That sort of thing. Ultimately, you sit there and try to think nothing. Thoughts arise. You let them go. Monsters from your unconscious rear up. You release them. You enter a zone of mental emptiness.

All of this is supposed to lead to a breakthrough—*satori,* enlightenment—which leads to pure consciousness and awareness without inner interpretation, which, in turn, gives rise to a sense that what you thought was reality is nothing more than an illusion. *The way is easy,* as one zen master put it. *Don't seek the truth. Just let go of all your opinions.*

Zen appealed to me because it seemed to offer a way to achieve what I had tried to achieve in childhood: a method of breaking free of the fog of daydreams and inner voices to see reality as it was. It was zen I had been trying to invent when I was eight years old, and now I had found it waiting for me. All I had to do was sit and breathe.

Now, of course, there is no competition in zen. You can't seek to do it better than anyone else. You can only sit. You can only breathe. There's no way to be good or bad at it. But oh brother, let me tell you, I was great at it! I could sit and breathe with the best of them. I cracked koans like they were walnuts. If you wanted to know the sound of one hand clapping, you only had to ask me. Your original face before you were born? No problem; I knew. I was an all-around World Champion Zazen Guy, no question. I'm convinced to this day that only an unreasoning prejudice against Western dilettantes kept me out of the Zen Hall of Fame.

The effect of meditation on me was wonderful too. At this time, due to budget cuts, I had been laid off from my job at the movie studio. I had found work writing news for a radio station located in Times Square. It was high-pressure work, churning out copy under half-hour deadlines from about three in the morning to around ten. When I was done for the day, I would come home and play with my daughter for an hour or so. Then I'd work for four hours at my own writing. Then I'd read from my stacks of books for two hours. Then I'd sleep a few hours; then I'd start the round again. I was constantly exhausted, constantly in motion, and often in severe pain: overdosing on coffee gave me an excruciating urinary infection that lasted for months.

But through my zen meditation, I remained focused and clearheaded as never before. The other newswriters and I would sometimes entertain ourselves between broadcasts by playing games of wastepaper basketball, tossing crumpled pieces of wire copy at the trash basket for a quarter a throw. Zen so sharpened my mind that I couldn't miss. I would frequently come home with my pockets bulging with change. It wasn't exactly enlightenment, but it was a legitimate ten- or fifteen-dollar add-on to my take-home pay. Finally, my colleagues caught on and the basketball games ended.

I would not only practice zen while sitting but also while walking around the city. I would clear my mind and focus on the buildings, the traffic, the trees, pavement, scenery, and faces—just as I had done as a boy trying to beat my daydream addiction. This time, with the aid of *zazen* breathing, I learned how to overcome the mind's resistance to emptiness. The city scenery grew clearer to me. I became more alert and aware.

Then one day, I was walking up Fifth Avenue. I was on that beautiful stretch along the border of Central Park where the hexagonal pavement stones lie shaded under the canopied branches of plane trees. I don't remember exactly where I was or where I was headed. Perhaps I was passing Temple Emmanuel on 65th Street. Perhaps it was the sight of that grand Romanesque Revival synagogue that suggested something to me. I don't know. I just know that all at once, two words spoke themselves into my consciousness:

No God.

And with that: *satori*! Or some dabbler's version of it anyway. Suddenly, my mind stopped. The chatter in my mind, the internal conversations, the reflections, the value judgments, the opinions, the daydreams, the very sense of myself—they all vanished on the instant. The static of consciousness shut off and the avenue came into focus like turning a lens. Colors became gloriously sharp and clear. The green of the budding leaves, the brown of the branches, the silver-gray of the paving stones, the blurred yellow of the passing cabs, the white clouds, the blue sky—they were so vibrantly and entirely *there* that I was breathless. I continued up Fifth Avenue awestruck, looking all around me, like a child at his first fair. Reality had become a wonderland.

Wherever I'd been headed, I forgot it now. I simply strolled on, enjoying the stridently vivid scenery. Whenever the clarity began to fade, whenever the noise of my mind started up again, I had only to reignite the experience with the same words that had begun it:

No God.

Soon I realized I was approaching the Metropolitan Museum of Art. How perfect. How beautiful the paintings would appear to my heightened consciousness. I went in and wandered the halls of the European galleries. Sure enough, the Christs and the Virgins and the pagan gods and the landscapes and the still-lifes seemed nearly three-dimensional with pure presence.

It was here in the museum, after another half hour or so, that the rush of awareness finally began to recede. The kick in the eye was over. Life became only life again.

What was I to make of this then? No God? Atheism? Was that the secret to enlightenment? It seemed the very antithesis of my epiphany in the delivery room and yet the experience was just as real. For an hour or so on Fifth Avenue and in the museum, I had stumbled onto something like the clarity and presence I had been seeking on my walk to school when I was eight years old. And it had all started with that one revelation: no God. Even after it was over, I only had to speak those words to myself, and I would get a taste of that clarity again.

Given that my idea of spirituality was not necessarily supernatural, atheism made a certain amount of sense to me at that time. After all, Freudian therapy was bringing me closer and closer to a kind of sanity and peace I had never dreamed of having. And there was no more confirmed atheist-materialist than Sigmund Freud. He had replaced the Trinity of Father, Son, and Holy Spirit with the Id, Ego, and Super-ego, three functions of the mind. He had replaced the fall of man with a story about a primal patricide in earliest times—that was how he explained our universal sense of guilt. He had essentially rewritten the story of Christianity into a new myth of the death and resurrection of our own flesh. For him, all our highest thoughts could be reinterpreted as expressions of our often thwarted and rechanneled erotic impulses.

If atheist Freud was leading me to sanity, and if the phrase *No God* was leading me to zen enlightenment, then it seemed integrity demanded I give up my agnostic uncertainty and declare myself an atheist.

So I tried it. I did. I put aside all thoughts of an outer spirit or of a living love beyond my own consciousness. I skewed my reading to favor atheist writing. Shaw, Kafka, Nietzsche, Freud and more Freud, and then more. The problem was, the atheist reasoning of these writers never held together for me.

I wanted even my daydreams to make sense, remember, and these writers did not. Even Freud, whom I loved so much, used flimsy logic often based on nothing more than his own opinions and a few isolated exchanges with his patients. Why was a made-up primal murder more convincing than Original Sin? Why were pleasure and pain the last words in human motivation? So much of human history proved there was more to us than that. It was simply that materialist prejudice at work again. It was not convincing on the merits.

Then, in my atheist reading, I came upon the writings of the Marquis de Sade. It marked a watershed in my thinking. Nowadays, "the divine Marquis" is sometimes depicted as a naughty rogue who enjoyed what the British call "a bit of the slap and tickle," a libertine who brought a needed dose of sexual freedom into a pinched and hypocritical era. That's not how I saw him at all. Sade—from whom we get the word *sadism*—was a violent psychopath who brutally tortured servants and prostitutes for his own pleasure. (When even the French imprison you for your sexual practices, you know you've crossed the line!) He was also a philosopher of genius.

Sade understood that if there is no God, there can be no ultimate morality. *There is nothing either good or bad but thinking makes it so.* Unlike Freud and other atheists, though, Sade followed mad Hamlet's logic with unswerving honesty. Without morality, he said, we are only responsible to our natures, and nature demands only that we pleasure ourselves in any way we like, the strong at the expense of the weak. "Nature, mother to us all, never speaks to us save of ourselves . . . prefer thyself, love thyself, no matter at whose expense," he declared. And then, with wonderful wit, he added: "Nature has endowed each of us with a capacity for kindly feelings: let us not squander them on others."[2] All of this, he illustrated with graphic passages of pornography depicting tortures, rapes, and murders in a way intended to be sexually arousing. And his work *is* arousing. It's also repulsive. And to my eyes, it's evil.

Here, at last, however, was an atheist whose outlook made complete logical sense to me from beginning to end. If there is no God, there is no morality. If there is no morality, the search for pleasure and the avoidance of pain are all in all and we should pillage, rape, and murder as we please. None of this pale, milquetoast atheism that says "Let's all do what's good for society." Why should I do what's good for society? What is society to me? None of this elaborate game-theory nonsense where we all benefit by mutual sacrifice and restraint. That only works until no one's looking; then I'll get away with what I can. If there is no God, there is no good, and sadistic pornography is scripture.

But the opposite is also true. That is, if we concede that one thing is morally better than another, it can only be because it is closer to an Ultimate Moral Good, the standard by which it's measured. An Ultimate Moral Good cannot just be an idea. It must be, in effect, a personality with consciousness and free will. The rain isn't morally good even though it makes the crops grow; a tornado that kills isn't morally evil— though it may be *an* evil for those in its way. Happy and sad events, from birth to death, just happen, and we ascribe moral qualities to them as they suit us or don't. But true, objective good and evil, in order to *be* good and evil, have to be aware and intentional. So an Ultimate Moral Good must be conscious and free; it must be God.

So we have to choose. Either there is no God and no morality whatsoever, or there is morality and God is real.

Either way makes sense, if you're speaking strictly about logic. I didn't reject Sade's outlook on logical grounds. I rejected it because I found it repulsive and I knew it wasn't true just as I know that one plus two always equals two plus one, though neither I nor anyone else can prove it. So, too, I know that a Nazi who tortures a child to death is less moral than a priest who gives a beggar bread—and that this is so even in a world that is all Nazis everywhere. In the chain of reasoning that took me finally to Christ, accepting this one axiom—that some actions are morally better than others—is the only truly nonlogical leap of faith I ever made. Hardly a leap really. Barely even a step. I know it's so. And those who declare they do not are, like Hamlet, only pretending.

After reading Sade, I abandoned atheism and returned to agnosticism. I couldn't quite bring myself to follow my own logic to its conclusions. That is, I couldn't quite bring myself to accept the existence of God. But I knew the road to hell when I saw it and I chose to go home by another way.

This left me trying to reconcile my zen revelation—*No God*—with the experience I had had in the delivery room of a living love outside myself. I began to wonder if perhaps the God my zen consciousness was rejecting was not the real God, but an internal one, the voices and opinions and illusions inside my head.

Because postmodernism is right in this at least: there is plenty we take for morality and truth that is mere prejudice. There is much we accept as wisdom that is only cultural habit. There is a great deal we mistake for reality that is simply a trick of the light. It is not a bad thing to clear the mind of the false god of our inner voices. That, I came to think, was the idea behind my *satori*.

In any case, during the months that followed my experience on Fifth Avenue, zen slowly lost its appeal for me. Sitting still and thinking of nothing, which had once sharpened my sense of life, now began to feel like an experience too much like death, a waste of precious moments that could be spent in action and vitality and self-awareness. Prolonged mental silence seemed a rehearsal for the grave. What's more, like postmodernism, *zazen* enforced its own conclusions. Meditate on nothing long enough, and you soon achieve inner nothingness. I assume if you meditated on turtles, it would be turtles all the way down.

And in fact, with an empty mind, a mind quieted through meditation, I had not found the world a Buddhistic illusion in the least. I had seen that world more clearly, that's all. That clarity—that was the fourth epiphany.

There was just one more to come.

⸺◦∞◦⸺

By now, my therapy was nearing its conclusion. My anger, depression, and hypochondria were all things of the past. I was working well and effectively. I was publishing success-fully. I was thriving economically. My home life was a joy. It had only been a few years since that moment when I sat in darkness contemplating suicide but both my interior and exterior lives were utterly transformed. I was ready to bring the therapeutic process to an end.

I faced this moment with both eagerness and regret. I had come to love my psychiatrist—my first and only mentor—as I had never loved any man. I'd been broken and he had healed me. It was clear we had developed a relationship beyond the normal therapeutic one. Under other circumstances we would surely have been friends. I knew I could come and visit him whenever I wanted. But it was going to be a sorrow to me to stop seeing him on a regular basis. Still, I was certain this was the right thing to do. It's true that the unexamined life is not worth living, but the unlived life is not worth examining. I needed to be free of ceaseless self-scrutiny in order to live.

I entered a kind of mourning period then. After that first therapeutic breakthrough when I had wept on the stairs, it had seemed to me the possibilities for renewal and personal transformation were infinite. But, of course, in the end you discover you are still yourself, no matter what. Some traits are in your nature, born with you. Some scars are written in your flesh indelibly, the signature of history. And some brokenness is simply inherent in the human condition. I was grieving over my limitations and the unchangeable past, mourning the ideal childhood I hadn't had, and the ideal parents my parents couldn't be.

I remember one day I was passing the building that had housed the radio station where my father worked most of my life. The station was gone now and the building was being remodeled. I went inside. I rode the elevator up to the floor where the radio station had been. The place had been gutted: walls removed, wires dangling from the ceiling, carpeting torn up. But smell is the sense of memory, and the place smelled the same, a unique smell radio stations had back then, a product, I suppose, of hermetic soundproofing and recirculated air. I drew in that smell and walked through the ruins. I could make out hallways and corners where I had once run and played as a child. I found the newsroom where the gruff reporters had stopped working long enough to kid around with a little boy. I stood in the space where my father's studio had been, where my father had stood at his microphone creating his amazing array of comical characters with their infinite variety of voices. I thought: *It should have been so much fun. We had everything. A roof over our heads and food to eat, an intact family, a father working at a job he enjoyed for good money; a fortunate life. Our house should have been filled with gratitude and charity and rejoicing.*

I knew I had to grieve the past, then let it go. Otherwise I would miss the gift these last few years had given me: a miraculous second chance to live out just such a life—a life of gratitude and charity and rejoicing—in a new family of my own.

I left the gutted station and the unchangeable truth of the past, and let them both trail off into the distance behind me.

There came a therapy session near the end where I was

talking about these things: dark things, sorrowful things, ugly things too. In the midst of it all, I began to laugh. I couldn't stop myself. I laughed and laughed, twisted and doubled over in the patient's chair, clutching my belly with one hand, wiping my eyes with the other. It wasn't hysterical laughter. It wasn't tragic laughter either. It wasn't even happy laughter really. It was just laughter, pure laughter, pure hilarity, pure mirth. Something—no, *everything*—struck me as funny. *Really* funny. Funny at its core, in its very nature: my past, my sorrow, my future, this moment; life; everything. I laughed and laughed. I couldn't stop.

Finally, coughing, giggling, gasping, I managed to force out the question: "Why . . . ? Why am I laughing? Why can't I stop laughing?"

And my psychiatrist, my beloved mentor, my beloved friend, said quietly, "Because this is who you really are. This is how you really see the world."

The fifth epiphany. The fifth fragment.

The truth of suffering. The wisdom of joy. The reality of love. The possibility of clear perception. The laughter at the heart of mourning.

I had them all now, all the pieces I needed. The five revelations that were really one revelation: *the presence of God.*

CHAPTER 12

THIS THING OF DARKNESS

I t was about ten years between the end of my therapy and the beginning of my faith. They were ten good years, taken all in all. I had come out of the therapeutic process a changed person, almost a different person. The delusions and tormenting thoughts of the past were gone. Ideas that had once seemed certain to me now looked like simple madness. My personality was so transformed I hardly recognized myself. Even little neurotic tics had somehow evaporated. Before, I had been a fearful flier. Afterward, I enjoyed flying so much I eventually earned a pilot's license. Before, I had been a nervous public speaker. Afterward, I spoke and performed with ease. I had not worked to fix these glitches particularly. They had just gone away as my fractured psyche was restructured into the man I was meant to be. I can take no credit for any of it really. It was the work of a brilliant doctor, a genius at his trade.

My only role had been to go on the journey. Now that it

was over, it was hard to believe it had ever happened. I sometimes likened the experience to hacking my way through an enchanted jungle. I slashed through entangling vines and clustered branches. I battled raging beasts and survived life-threatening dangers. And when at last I broke out into the fair country on the other side, I looked behind me and saw the jungle was gone, nothing but open plains as far as the eye could see, as if none of the obstacles and monsters had ever really been there in the first place.

My world was full now. I did the work I loved. My family prospered. Ellen and I had a second child, a son, Spencer. Like our daughter, Faith, he proved the truth of one of our family slogans: "More love, more life." He was a cheerful addition to the clan too. Once, when he was about three years old, he sat playing in a sunbeam on the back porch of our weekend house in Connecticut. He looked up into the light and said aloud, "Thank you, sun, for shining on me." At this point, I felt pretty much the same way.

There was a time when I used to ask myself why it took so long—a full decade—before I faced up to the conclusions of my own reasoning and experience and accepted what should have been so obvious: the presence of God in my life. But I think I know the answer now. In part, it had to do with coming to trust this new mentally healthy self of mine. It took a while before I was fully convinced that my delusions were gone for good, that my outlook was sound and the things I believed about the world around me were true. It took a while, too, before I grew confident in my self-education and felt competent to disagree with the sages of postmodernity.

And there was something else, something more, a final problem I had to resolve in my own mind before I could move forward in my thinking and in my beliefs. I didn't realize it at the time, but looking back I see it clearly. Before I could free myself to accept my latent spiritual conclusions, I had to think through the issue of Western anti-Semitism. In the next few years, I would write three novels that helped me find my way.

For me, this problem was personal. Western anti-Semitism created a dilemma in my mind, which was this: Through my years of reading, I had come to believe, as I do still, that the nations of Europe from, say, the Renaissance to the First World War, had produced more of mankind's greatest artistic achievements than any others. I know this is now an unpopular sentiment. Some people condemn it as triumphalist. Some even call it racist. Some consider it merely impolite. In fact, it sometimes seems to me the entire postmodern assault on the concept of truth has been staged to avoid just this conclusion: some cultures are simply more productive than others and the high culture of Europe has been the most impressive so far. It's as if, in the aftermath of the racist cataclysm of the Holocaust, Western thinkers have grown so skittish around the idea of racism they will do anything to avoid naming their culture as superior to others, even if it means avoiding the evidence of their own eyes.

I despise racism. It's in conflict with everything I feel and everything I believe. But for me, the greatness of European culture is neither a racial issue nor a moral one, just an observational truth. As the discoveries and calculus of Newton are more important scientific breakthroughs than anything that came before or since, as the Constitution of the American founders is the most profound piece of distilled political wisdom in all history, it makes simple sense that the artistic culture that underlay those advances, the culture that includes the poetry of Shakespeare and Keats, the music of Bach and Mozart, the painting and sculpture of Michelangelo and Raphael, and the novels of Cervantes, Zola, Tolstoy, and Dickens was somehow better, richer, and deeper than any other culture that has ever existed on earth.

This has nothing to do with whether these people were nice or decent or did good things. It only concerns the objects they made and left behind. I don't think it's a matter of mere taste either. No matter what the popular thinking is, I can't convince myself that the greatness of a work of art lies in the appreciation of the observer. I believe art does something. I believe it records and preserves the inner experience of being human. I believe some art does this better and more honestly and more completely than other art, whether I happen to enjoy it or not. I'd rather read Raymond Chandler than Gustave Flaubert, but Flaubert is greater.

So I thought—and think—that the beauty and truth of man's inner life—the beauty and truth of the human spirit—were recorded in the artworks of high Europe more consistently than in any others. This, in turn, gave me a deep respect, bordering on awe, for the underlying philosophy that shaped and informed these works: the Christian worldview.

But if Christianity was the spiritual light that shone within the greatest art of Europe, it was also the dark face of its philosophical shadow: Europe's hatred of the Jews.

I am a Jew. Even now, even in Christ—I would say never more so. I'm proud of this, belligerently proud. Mine is a uniquely great people. We represent about .2 percent of the world. Not 2 percent. Point two. Statistically almost zero. Yet make a list of the most consequential individuals who have ever lived and Jews will be thick among them, from Moses, David, Jesus, and St. Paul to Karl Marx, Sigmund Freud, and Albert Einstein. Around one-fifth of all Nobel Prizes have gone to people of Jewish heritage, more if you only count the science prizes. Point 2 percent of the population. About thirteen million souls. There are single cities with more people in them than that.

And these Jews, these thinkers of thoughts, these writers of books, these doctors, inventors, entertainers, tradesmen— these are the single most despised and put upon people on the face of the planet, bar none. In an age where victimhood carries with it a sick sort of glamour, where any number of interest groups demand to be proclaimed the most oppressed—too late! The Jews have won that thorny crown going away. From the Roman destruction of Jerusalem to the ceaseless pogroms and exiles of the European Middle Ages, from the Holocaust to the current attempts to isolate and destroy the state of Israel, the Jews are the perennial victimized Others of the West.

No one today would call Jew-hatred Christian, but as Christianity shaped every good thing about Western culture so it shaped this bad thing as well. "The Jews killed Christ." This was the central Christian teaching on the subject of my people for centuries. It's not even an English sentence really. It's like that Noam Chomsky formulation that makes grammatical sense but is semantically ridiculous: *Colorless green ideas sleep furiously.* It's like saying *The whites held slaves* or *The blacks rioted in Los Angeles* or *The Germans killed the Jews.* Did some poor shnook who wasn't there do it? Did the guilt seep into his cells through some racial radiation and then flow down through his DNA into his children yet unborn? It's a colorless green idea, all right, and it has slept furiously in the mind of man for way too long.

So for me, who loved Western culture so much, who spent his life studying it, and who even worked in it in my small way, the question was this: If Jew hatred was Western Christendom's shadow self, were the two inseparable? Were the two really one? Was the great art and culture of Europe— the art I felt best led a man to wisdom—so infected with this poison that to feed on the one was to die of the other?

Even when I was a young man, these questions bothered me. Anti-Semitism was there in many of the books I loved so much. In Hemingway's *The Sun Also Rises*, there was the puling character Robert Cohn with his "Jewish superiority" and his "sad Jewish face." There was Shylock in Shakespeare; Fagin in Dickens; the horrible Meyer Wolfsheim in *The Great Gatsby.* So many bent, weak, whiny, grasping, dishonest Jewish characters in Western fiction, so many of them identified only as "The Jew." I understood these works reflected attitudes of their times. Some might even have given fair depictions of true-to-life figures the authors had met. Still, these writers were my culture heroes and, more to the point, this culture was my culture, and for much of its history, my people were its central image of the despicable.

And then, of course, there was the Holocaust, the systematic extermination of Europe's Jews by one of its greatest nations. It was as if, as its great culture came to its conclusion, Europe was transformed into its own shadow, spiraling down to die in the darkness at its core.

My father was obsessed with the Holocaust. He was convinced that at any moment it would begin again, right here in America. Any cultural development that worried him seemed to him the prelude to the mass extermination of American Jews. Any politician he disagreed with was a Nazi. Was there an upsurge in conservatism? A call for more law and order? Even a rise in patriotic feeling? As my father saw it, this meant the country was only one step away from rebuilding the death camps at some secret location, no doubt somewhere in the ever-so-threatening midwest.

A lot of Jews of my father's generation felt something like this for a while after World War II. It was an understandable reaction to the trauma of having lived through the Holocaust era. But as time wore on and other Jews recovered, my father's fears grew more fixed and pathological. He developed an almost comical knee-jerk reaction to nearly every event in the news. It only took some blowhard getting elected dog catcher, and he'd be at it again: *Here it comes. This is it. Hitler's back. We're all dead men.* In the midst of American peace and plenty, he saw the storm clouds of slaughter forever gathering above us. He even kept a collection of gold bars hidden in one of his bedroom closets in case we needed to bribe the guards at the Canadian border as we escaped from blood-soaked tyranny to freedom like the von Trapp family at the end of *The Sound of Music.*

From childhood on, I could see that Dad was irrational on this point. Still, his paranoia kept the issue of anti-Semitism always before me. As my love of European culture grew—and as its wisdom drew me subconsciously toward its Christly center—I began to question whether its bigotries were central to its vision. Was the Holocaust inherent in the Sistine Chapel? Was it inevitable from the moment Michelangelo's Adam extended his hand toward the hand of God?

With the crisis of my madness over, with my work going well and my life going well, I began to study the Holocaust with a rigor and clarity I'd never really had before. For months I read the books, watched the documentaries, and suffered through the resulting nightmares almost every night.

The Holocaust is not the worst thing that ever happened in history. It's worse even than that. It lives in a darkness beyond history. It's the Marquis de Sade's philosophy brought to fruition: hell on earth. The Holocaust is beyond art too. It's the opposite of art, the opposite of Keats's "Ode to Autumn," the opposite of a world imbued with and understood through the human spirit. Stories of humanity during the event—even true stories like *Schindler's List* or *The Hiding Place*—are so anomalous as to amount to sentimental lies. There was no humanity, and so there can be no true fictions about it, no paintings, no music. I've visited those death camps. Art has no power there. Even the birds don't sing.

It may seem paradoxical, but I began to plan a novel about this very fact—about the fact that the whole Western idea of beauty and art was called into question by the truth of the Holocaust. It was my way of dealing with the issue that was haunting me: whether Western Jew-hatred undermined the whole cultural enterprise of which I, a Jew, was now a small part.

About this time, we left New York City and moved to England. I had never enjoyed New York much. Now that I could afford it, I wanted to get away, put some distance between me and my parents, and see the world. On top of this, I was beginning to find the growing American mania for so-called political correctness oppressive. In Manhattan, at least, PC had begun to curtail and poison nearly every intellectual conversation. You could hardly express an opinion without finding yourself condemned for it, especially if the opinion was obviously true. It was as if people thought reality could be lied into submission. If you would only say the world was what it wasn't it would magically become what you said it was.

One night, I stunned an entire dinner gathering into embarrassed silence by making the shocking observation that boys and girls are different. This self-evident truth was now a sexist blasphemy. As we walked out of the restaurant, I turned to my wife in sardonic disgust and said, "We're leaving the country, baby." Soon afterward, we did.

We found a flat in South Kensington, London. Moving to London seemed the easiest option. I had some friends there, fellow writers and publishers, and I could speak the language more or less. I only intended to stay for a year, put some breathing space between me and America, get some perspective on my homeland. But I fell in love with the place, the city first and then the entire country.

It really was like love, too, the whole experience—it was just like a romance. I couldn't stay away from London. I couldn't take my eyes off her. Down the hidden cobbled streets and past the stern Victorian piles, along the ancient Thames and out into the brick-and-chimney suburbs and the rolling countryside—I walked and walked everywhere, rapt and fascinated. The sense of deep history seemed to flow up out of the ground into my shoe soles and all through me. It made me feel peaceful somehow just to know so much civilization had been where I was now. I woke up every morning happy, eager to be near it, really just like in a romance. When our year there was over, I found I couldn't leave. We ended up staying in London for seven years.

But at the same time I was falling in love with both the city and the country, I could not help but notice the anti-Semitism everywhere.

I met in Great Britain some of the kindest, most decent, most civilized, cultured, and witty people I have ever known. But the open racialism of the British startled my innocent American sensibilities. At a literary party I attended about a month after our move, a man buttonholed me and, in all seriousness, began to instruct me in the differences among the peoples of the Isles. The Welsh were cheap, the Scots were stupid, the Irish drunk, and so on. Finally, irritated at his open bigotry, I drawled at him in my best Ugly American fashion, "This country's the size of Oregon, man, how different can y'all be?" Well, at least it ended the conversation.

To be fair, for the most part, the English hated other races only just a little more than they hated their own. That is, in general their racialism targeted everybody alike, including themselves. Whenever I told one of my British friends how much I loved their country, they invariably responded with a startled, "Why?" I had to explain to them why it was a great place and how they were a great people.

But the British hostility toward the Jews was different. It was special. It had the heat of fever to it. I had lived thirty-five years in America. I had traveled through almost every state, spoken to every class and kind of person, and I had had virtually no experience of true anti-Semitism, none. Now, suddenly, I found myself sitting in London restaurants and clubs and overhearing normal, civilized people ranting out loud about the evildoing of "the Jews." The Jews caused wars. The Jews ruined economies. The BBC news stories about Israel were so slanted they amounted to hate speech. Even friends— good friends, good people—made remarks that appalled me. "The Jews secretly run this country." "A Jew can never really be an Englishman." "Jews cling to eye-for-eye justice instead of Christian mercy." And so on.

It seemed every other person I met would ask me, "What sort of name is Klavan?" At first, I thought they wanted to know about my family background. I would launch into some cheerful explanation about how my people had come over from eastern Europe and Austria, how some official at Ellis Island had probably changed our name from Klavansky or whatever. But soon I realized what they were really asking me. After a while, whenever someone said, "What sort of name is Klavan?" I would respond quickly, sharply, "I'm a Jew," and then watch them blush and stutter.

Whenever I heard an anti-Semitic comment, I answered it in my blunt, obstreperous American way. Nonetheless, over the years I started to feel a kind of racial awareness I'd never felt before. For the first time in my life, I felt conspicuous—and conspicuously Jewish—as if I was wearing my heritage on my face. It was the faintest taste—just the faintest—of what it must be like to be black in a majority white country.

So I was not only asking myself questions about my love of Western culture in light of that culture's core anti-Semitism, I was living those questions out to some degree: loving England, loving Britain, loving Europe—all the while seeing and hearing evidence of its enduring shadow self.

I mentioned earlier how I visited Munich one Christmastime, how I went to the Christmas Market in Marienplatz—Mary's Square. There was a light snow falling on the square's massive Christmas tree. There were carolers singing on the balcony of the ornate neo-gothic city hall. There were red-cheeked children ogling the wooden toys and glass ornaments on display everywhere. And there was that smell of baked goods that carried my memories back to Mina's house and Mina's Christmas so that I had the visceral sense that I was home.

But earlier that day, Ellen and I had paid a visit to Dachau, the notorious Nazi concentration camp just outside the city, close enough so that every adult Munchner must have known that it was there. Dachau was not a "death camp," and many of the prisoners tormented and killed in it weren't Jews. But toward the end of the war the Nazis did install their signature gas chambers in the place, though they were never used. I had seen countless pictures of these murder machines in the books I had been reading, but these were the first I ever saw in reality and up close. The moment I laid eyes on them, I had the strangest experience. I heard a terrible noise nearby me, a strangled sob of grief and anguish. I looked over one shoulder and then the other to see who had cried out. Several seconds passed before I realized the noise had come from my own throat.

I was a man who felt at home in the living Christmas card of Marienplatz. I was also a man whose people had been slaughtered wholesale by this country. Were these two men, both inside me, so alienated from each other that they could never be reconciled?

I began to write the novel I'd been planning back in America, the first of the three novels that helped me through this impasse: *Agnes Mallory*. It's about the friendship between a corrupt Jewish politician named Harry Bernard and Agnes, a Jewish sculptress who works in wood. The daughter of a

Holocaust survivor, Agnes is haunted by the fact that she had a half sister who died in the camps before she was born. She can't reconcile her desire to create something beautiful in the Western tradition with the West's mass slaughter of her people. She feels that the very concept of Western beauty itself has been called into question.

When Harry's corruption is exposed in the New York City scandals of the 1980s, he runs away and hides out with Agnes in her secluded Vermont cottage. As his friendship with Agnes becomes a romance, Harry finds himself confronting a mystery. Every day he hears Agnes chiseling away in her studio. Every dawn, she throws a log on the wood-burning stove and goes out for a swim in the nearby river. But the only work of hers he ever sees are the beautiful statues that lie rotting in a ghostly valley of dead elms in the forest around them.

Agnes has discarded the statues there because she feels she cannot sculpt an image that is at once beautiful and at the same time embodies the dreadful truth of her culture, the truth exposed in the death camps of World War II. Ultimately, to his horror, Harry discovers what's going on. Every day Agnes is re-creating a fabulously beautiful sculpture of her lost half sister—and every dawn she is destroying the sculpture in the wood-burning stove. It is the only way she knows how to capture the essence of the Holocaust in art. The rest of the story spins out from this act of creative purity and madness.

To my great sorrow, I could not find a publisher for this novel in America. It came out in England but only became available in the United States some twenty years later when I cajoled an e-publisher into re-issuing it with a number of my early thrillers. Baffled and frustrated by my inability to sell in my home country what I knew to be a very good piece of work, I showed the *Agnes* manuscript to a friend of mine. He was a highly perceptive and intelligent writer, widely read, with a PhD from Yale. "Don't you understand?" he said to me, with some exasperation. "Your thinking is going in completely the opposite direction to the intellectual trends of our times." I don't think even he knew how right he was.

Maybe if I could have published the novel at home, I would have felt a sense of closure and let the matter rest. But I don't think so. Something was going on inside me below the level of consciousness. The epiphanies and revelations of my therapeutic years were continuing to do their work even without my knowledge. I thought I was an agnostic for life. I thought I had accepted what I had come to call "The Burden of Unknowing." It wasn't so. I was changing inside. I should have seen it in my next novel, the second of these three, *True Crime.*

True Crime is a thriller about faith and doubt. It tells how an innocent Christian on Missouri's death row faces the existential fact of injustice and death while a cynical atheist reporter prays for a miracle as he tries to save him at the last minute. As the hour of execution nears and the prisoner's faith begins to crumble, a pastor visits him. The pastor tells the prisoner that, whether he lives or dies, his religious vision has to be big enough to include the injustice and suffering of human existence.

"You want to believe in God," the pastor says, "you're

gonna have to believe in a God of the *sad* world." When I reread this passage now, it seems to me my heart was talking to itself, teaching itself again the hard lesson it had learned in a darkened room back in Manhattan: even in the realms of faith and history, maybe especially in the realms of faith and history, sometimes you just have to play in pain.

Still, the matter of my own relationship to faith and history remained unsettled. So when I began to plan my next novel, the final one in this series, I returned to the dilemma that was bothering me. With that, I began the single strangest writing experience of my life and produced my weirdest novel, aptly named *The Uncanny*.

To this day, I don't know whether *The Uncanny* is any good or not. I know some people love it; but more, I suspect, hate it—hate it a lot. "This book stank," is one of the more concise reviews of it on Amazon.com. I'd like to have the book back to write again from the beginning. I even tried once to refashion the core of the story into a play. In doing so, I felt I came closer to what I would have liked the plot to be. But I've never had the play produced, so I don't know if it would work any better with an audience than the novel did.

What I do know is that writing the book changed me. It was as if, even in the happy years that followed my therapy, there was one more knot inside me that needed to be untied and somehow writing *The Uncanny* did the job. I don't believe in writing as a form of self-exploration. I don't write for myself. I write to tell stories, communicate a vision. The reader is the point of the exercise, not me. But whenever I think of *The*

Uncanny—which is often—whenever I scold myself for writing a book I knew very few people would enjoy, I can't help but remind myself that this was the book that undid that final knot inside me and freed my mind at last for faith. I chalk it up to an act of God.

The core of the narrative concerns Richard Storm, a shallow but lovable producer of horror films, and a fully assimilated American Jew. (His father, a small-time actor, was originally named Morgenstern, but John Wayne gave him the stage name Storm. When you have been "christened" by John Wayne, you are about as assimilated as you can get!) When Storm discovers he might be dying, he comes to England, searching for the source of his favorite Victorian ghost story. His hope is that he will discover something uncanny on which he can base a faith in the afterlife. Instead, he finds himself tracing the story back through a series of related tales from various time periods. At last, he discovers the story's origin in a true tale of a twelfth-century anti-Semitic atrocity. It turns out the very wellspring of the culture he loves is imbued with a hatred for his race.

The novel has a strong strain of satire. It is full of parody references to other novels, especially those like Henry James's *The Ambassadors*, that deal with the differences between American and European cultures. Its running joke is that the heavy, morbid European sense of the burden of history transforms Storm's shallow but happy American ignorance into a kind of accidental wisdom. In a nod to Faulkner's famous dictum, "The past is never dead. It's not even past," Storm goofily but rather profoundly asks, "If the past isn't past, what is?" With that attitude to guide him, even in the light of the European murder of the Jews—even in the face of his own death—Storm retains a childlike American faith in the power of each new soul to start the world again.

The plot of *The Uncanny* entangles various European legends into one big vast and eternal conspiracy, but somehow, the writing of it untangled me. Every day as I worked, I felt my mood elevated, sometimes almost to the point of mysticism. Sometimes I would leave my office with a powerful sense of the great unity behind and beyond the minute particulars of life. It was as if I was glimpsing again that sea of love I had seen and nearly entered at my daughter's birth. It reminded me of the sense I'd had then that our mortal lives were just incarnate metaphors, that we are stories being told about the living love that created us and sustains us. It made me wonder if maybe that was true of all history. Maybe all of history's beauty and bloodshed was a story not about pleasure and pain and power but about humanity's relationship with an unseen spirit of love. We yearned for that spirit but we feared and hated it, too, because when it shone its terrible light on us, we saw ourselves as we were, broken and shameful, far from what the spirit of love had made us. Maybe all our wars and rapes and oppressions were just our attempts to extinguish that light and silence that story.

The very moment I put the last period on *The Uncanny*'s last sentence, I knew the work had done something to me. I could sense the change right away, and as the days went by I became certain of it. The proof was this:

There had been one annoying neurotic symptom that had

remained with me after my therapy. Every now and then, I would find myself in an internal, imaginary argument with my father. This was not my real father anymore, of course. He and I had come to a distant but peaceable understanding with each other. This was what the psychologists call an *introject*, the idea of my father that lived in my own mind, and now spoke to me as a part of myself. When these arguments with introject Dad got started in my head, they would become compulsive, addictive. I would get a rich, sickly pleasure out of rehearsing them over and over. By an effort of will, I had trained myself to stop them as soon as they began, but it bothered me that the old man, even in imagination, still had this sort of power over me.

But the moment I finished *The Uncanny*, the internal arguments stopped, never to return. As the weeks went on, I knew I had become free in a new way, a special and uncommon way. With William Faulkner, I understood that the past is never dead, but like Richard Storm, I had now come to feel—truly feel—that the past was past. If the past isn't past, what is?

In this new mental freedom, I came to see that the dilemma I had been wrestling with—my love of a culture that had done so much evil and yet produced such lasting beauty— was only my personal portion of the greater human paradox. We are never free of the things that happen. Every evil weaves itself into the fabric of history, never to be undone. Yet at the same time—at the very same time—each of us gets a new soul with which to start the world again.

It would take a few more years, but I would finally come to understand that I had, in effect, reinvented the doctrines of Original Sin and Salvation. This paradox, my paradox, was the riddle solved by the incarnation and death and resurrection of Jesus Christ. He offered a spiritual path out of the history created by Original Sin and into the newborn self remade in his image. It is the impossible solution to the impossible problem of evil. All reason says it can't be so. But it's the truth that sets us free.

I would come to feel that the West's enduring hatred of the Jews only made sense in light of the truth of both that indelible sin and that miraculous salvation. In the Bible, the Jews are "chosen" in the sense that God selects them as his doorway back into the world after the separation of the Fall. As such, they represent all people everywhere, a microcosm of what we are like in relationship to God. Seen in that context, the statement "the Jews killed Christ," begins to make sense. It means we all killed Christ, all humanity, to the last woman and man. To limit that killing to the Jews is a simple act of racist denial and willed blindness, an attempt to say, "They did it, Lord, not us; not us."

The Holocaust was the crucifixion compulsively reenacted on a grand scale: an attempt to kill God's people in order to extinguish the Light of the World that shows us as we are. Sigmund Freud called this the "return of the repressed," a concept he discusses, not so oddly enough, in his essay "The Uncanny." According to this idea, we bury the trauma and guilt of our past—in this case, the murder of God—and then we keep reenacting that trauma helplessly, in this case through the murder of God's people. The things we can't face come back and back to us, shaping our actions, getting bigger and bigger, until finally we either face the cause of them or they destroy us. Europe, in the end, was destroyed. It was their great culture that died in those death camps. The Jews—and their God—live on.

There are some people who say that an evil as great as the Holocaust is proof there is no God. But I would say the opposite. The very fact that it *is* so great an evil, so great that it defies any material explanation, implies a spiritual and moral framework that requires God's existence. More than that. The Holocaust was an evil that only makes sense if the Bible is true, if there is a God, if the Jews are his people, and if we would rather kill him and them than truly know him, and ourselves.

CHAPTER 13

MY CONVERSION

One winter's night near the end of the last millennium, I lay in bed reading a novel. I was in midlife at this point, around forty-five years old; still living in London, in a pleasant block of flats on the border of South Kensington and Earl's Court. It was around midnight. My wife was asleep beside me. My teenage daughter was asleep in her room down the hall. My nine-year-old son was asleep in his room beside hers.

The novel I was reading was a sea story by Patrick O'Brian. It was one of his wonderful series of adventure novels set during the Napoleonic Wars. The series featured a British naval captain named Jack Aubrey and his friend, a surgeon named Stephen Maturin. Like Holmes and Watson or Jeeves and Wooster, Maturin and Aubrey are a mind-body pair. Aubrey is a bluff, handsome, go-straight-at-'em warrior. Maturin is a dark, ugly, sometimes tormented philosopher. Making my way through the series, I had become emotionally invested in both these make-believe men. But Maturin, I came to feel, often acts as a stand-in for the author, so I identified with him a bit more.

I don't remember exactly which of the books I was reading that night. But just as I was starting to doze off, I reached a scene in which Maturin also went to bed. O'Brian described him climbing wearily into his hammock on whatever ship he was in at the time. Then, with a single sentence, the author told how the Catholic surgeon said a brief prayer just before he fell asleep.

The scene came at a break in the chapter. It was a good place to stop for the night. As I lay the book by the clock on my bedside table, I thought to myself, *Well, if Maturin can pray, then so can I.*

It seemed an almost random thought, but it wasn't really. For some time I had been wondering whether I might let go of my agnostic resistance and allow myself to believe what I knew deep down I had come to believe. The logic of good and evil supported me in my half-buried faith. So did the undeniable reality of certain inward experiences: the experiences of beauty and truth and of love above all. My old objections— that faith might be a crutch in hard times or some other form of neurosis—were simply no longer plausible. The hard times had been over for quite a while. And bizarre as it was even to myself, I was not neurotic anymore. I was at least as sane as any man I knew.

As I closed my eyes, I thought very quickly of the people I loved tucked up in their beds all around me. I thought of the life I had—a life of writing, and family, and traveling the world. The life I'd always longed for. I thought of the happiness and sanity and inner peace I'd never expected and which was still such a daily visceral pleasure to me.

And I prayed. I prayed: *Thank you, God.* And then, like Maturin, I fell asleep.

It was, looking back on it, a small and even a prideful prayer: an intellectual's hesitant experiment, three words intended to test the waters of belief without any real mental commitment.

God's response, on the other hand, was wildly generous, an act of extravagant grace.

I woke up the next morning and was immediately aware that everything had changed. I had changed—the tenor of my imagination had shifted—and that had changed everything. I somehow knew right away it was the prayer that had done it and I soon saw what it was that the prayer had done. There was a sudden clarity and brightness to familiar objects and to the details of my wife's, my daughter's, and my son's beloved faces. But it wasn't just that. I often had such moments of heightened clarity these days. This was different. This was more. The world was not merely bright but also full. The coffee in the mug, the hand that set the mug in front of me, the eyes that looked at me, those green eyes I had loved as if forever—they were alive suddenly with meaning and value. They were imbued with what they meant to me. I *felt* what they meant to me with a new power. My love of them. My pleasure in them. My joy.

As I walked outside, as I made my way to my office through the quaint and lovely back streets of South Ken, the pastel townhouses and iron gates and stone steeples from another age all presented themselves to me suffused with this new quality: my own delight in them.

What is this? I asked myself. *What is this thing?*

And I answered back: *I am feeling the joy of my joy.*

That was it. The joy of my joy. The life of my life spoken back to me by the world. That was what my three-word prayer—*Thank you, God*—had won for me. In even the little light of even that little gratitude, I was finally seeing existence as it was, not as an empty natural process of birth and death but as the miraculous creation of a personal Spirit: I AM THAT I AM. The joy of my joy was what I had felt slipping away from me when I was eight years old, what I had tried so hard to see again, both then and later through zen meditation. But I had made a mistake: I had tried to do it alone.

You cannot know yourself alone, any more than you can see your own face without a mirror. This was what I had learned in therapy. As my belief in Freud's insights had crumbled over the years, I had wondered: If Freud was wrong in his most basic assumptions, how had Freudian therapy transformed my life so completely? The answer was the love. It wasn't the theories or interpretation of therapy that had redeemed me. It was the love. I had loved my mentor and he loved his patients. He had been able to reflect me back to myself because of his wisdom, but he had been able to reflect me truly because of his love.

So it was now with all the world and God. Reality is the same for everyone, but your experience of reality is yours alone. You cannot know that experience fully by yourself, you cannot *experience* that experience fully by yourself. It must be reflected back to you by its source, its creator, and only his love can reflect it back to you as it actually is. You cannot know the truth about the world until you know God loves you, because that is the truth about the world.

In saying my little prayer, I had finally opened my heart to reality. And I could finally—finally—feel the joy of my joy.

Well, in any case, I know a good thing when I see one! Clearly, for whatever reason, this prayer business was powerful stuff. I tried it again that day and again the next day and again the next. Each day the prayers grew longer and more detailed. Five minutes long, ten minutes, fifteen, now and then even twenty or thirty. But sure enough, every day the result was the same: a refreshed awareness of gratitude, a full consciousness of life and meaning, the joy of my joy.

Prayer became my daily practice. I would do it once a day, while walking to work or when alone in my office. It wasn't easy at first. I didn't have any religious tradition to turn to. I had to learn how to pray from scratch. Anyway, I wasn't interested in reciting other people's prayers, no matter how time-tested or beautiful they might be. If I was going to talk to God, I wanted to talk to him directly and in my own way.

But what was I supposed to say? What words was I supposed to use? Did my prayers have to be pious and formal or could I just rap and jabber as I would with anyone? And who was this God I was talking to? Was it the old guy with the long, white beard from the Sistine Chapel? Was it some vague New Age spirit without a face or personality? Or was it really just me? Was I just talking to myself, practicing some elaborate form of self-therapy?

I didn't know. I wasn't sure. After a lifetime of agnosticism, it was all very new. I had to feel my way.

I experimented. I tried different kinds of prayers. Could I ask for stuff? I wondered. Did it have to be good stuff? Serious stuff? Moral stuff? Did I have to pray for world peace? Or could I put in a request to win the lottery? The truth was—just being honest—I didn't care a fig about world peace. I didn't believe there would ever be world peace, the world being what it was, so the only reason I could think to pray for it was to show God what a great guy I was—and then maybe he'd let me win the lottery. But, in fact, I found to my surprise that deep down I didn't really care if I won the lottery either. I wasn't rich, but I had enough money. I had my work, my love, the bright world. I was ambitious for more, but I wanted to earn it, not have it flashed down on me out of the sky. So did I even *want* to ask God for anything? It was complicated.

That said, there was one important aspect of prayer that was clear to me right away. Whoever God was, he was unlikely to be fooled by any show of righteousness or even seriousness on my end. If this really was God I was talking to, I could be pretty sure he already knew my corrupt and hilarious heart. There was nothing to hide and no point in trying to hide it. I might as well tell him everything as straight as I could.

At first, I overreacted to this idea. I became overstrict in my honesty, just as I had been when I first entered therapy. I would try to parse every selfish motive behind even my most kindly petitions. After all, if you're praying for the starving children of Africa in the secret hope God will be impressed with you and give you a hot new car, why not skip the hypocrisy and ask for the car directly? It's not as if you're fooling anyone.

After a while, though, it began to seem to me that I was thinking too much about perfect truth-telling. It was a waste of prayer time. The human heart is so steeped in self-deception that it can easily outrun its own lies. It can use even meticulous honesty as a form of dishonesty, a way of saying to God, "Look how honest I am." So I let it go. I let it all go. I just flung wide the gates to the sorry junkyard of my soul and let God have a good look at the whole rubble-strewn wreck of it. Then I went ahead and told him my thoughts as plainly as I knew how.

I went on praying. I prayed every day. Every day, the joy of my joy grew more present to me. And God became more present to me as well.

There is an old play called *The Ruling Class* by Peter Barnes. I saw the movie version when I was seventeen or so. It's about a mad English lord who decides that he's really Jesus Christ. How does he know? "Simple," he says. "When I pray to Him, I find I am talking to myself." That's a clever line. But I had the opposite experience. As the days, then weeks, then months and ultimately years of prayer continued, I slowly became convinced that I was not talking to myself at all. The revelations, the insights, the guidance, and the gifts that were given to me through prayer were all too unexpected. The presence of the Other was simply too real. I wasn't crazy, after all. Not anymore. I'd put a lot of work into making sure of that.

My other internal experiences were sound enough. My love lasted. My friendships were true. I could tell the difference between beauty and a poke in the eye.

And I could feel God there. I could feel myself growing closer to him as I prayed. I could feel myself coming to know him better. He was not like anyone else I had ever met. He was certainly not like my parents, no matter what Freud said. Every time I projected my father's traits or my mother's traits onto him, I soon discovered I had strayed from his reality. That wasn't him at all. And he wasn't like myself either. Whenever I imposed my own judgments or moral understanding on him, I invariably found that I had falsely limited his capacity for forgiveness and love. Despite my attempts to get him to conform to my preconceived philosophical notions of him— despite my occasional attempts to manipulate him into being who I wanted him to be—I found I could not change him, nor force him from his grace. It was he, rather, who changed me. It was I who began to try to move in his direction.

Five years of prayer went by. Like any five-year span, it included both good times and bad. There were successes and failures, pleasures and sufferings, some births and the deaths of more than one person I loved. There were periods of great peace and contentment and periods of struggle. There were even a few periods of shattering grief. I prayed through all of it, and the result of my prayers was always the same.

Joy. The joy of my joy. There through everything. A shocking sense of vitality and beauty present in both happiness and in the midst of pain. The only thing I can think to compare this experience to is the experience of an excellent story—reading a great novel, say, or watching a great movie. The scene before you might be a happy one or a sad one. You might feel uplifted or you might feel heartbroken or you might feel afraid. But whatever you feel, you're still loving the story. Through prayer, I came to experience both pleasure and sorrow in something like that way. In God, the life of the flesh became the story of the spirit. I loved that story, no matter what.

During this time, we moved back to America. It was odd. The goodness of living overseas just ran out somehow. For six and a half years, I had immersed myself in the life of Britain. My children had gone to British schools, my friends had been British, I followed British news and politics, watched British shows on television, and learned a good deal about British history and customs. Then, almost overnight, without thinking about it or knowing why, I changed. I found myself frequenting ex-patriate bars, reading American newspapers, sitting up late at night and leaning close to my computer to try to hear baseball games on the staticky broadcasts of early Internet radio. I knew it was time to go home.

At first, Ellen and I just assumed we would return to the East Coast. It was the place we knew best. We traveled back there a few times, scouting around our old haunts for a place to live in suburban New York or nearby Connecticut.

Then one day, as we were driving through the area looking at houses for sale, my wife said to me, "You know, every time we go house hunting, you get kind of grumpy."

It was true. I considered it. "It's because I don't want to come back here," I told her. "It feels like the past to me."

"Well then, let's not. Let's go somewhere new. Let's go to California!" she said brightly.

I thought about it only a second. Then I shrugged. "Okay."

It made sense actually. A couple of my novels were being made into movies then, and some of the studios were hiring me from time to time as a screenwriter. I'd never particularly wanted to be in the movie business, but I found now that I enjoyed it. After all the solitary years of fiction writing, it was a pleasure to work with other people. Los Angeles was where the business was, so we headed in that direction. We didn't want to raise our kids in the city, so we settled in Montecito, just outside of Santa Barbara, about eighty miles north of LA.

It was there, when these five years of prayer were over, that I drove up into the mountains one morning. It had been, as I say, a time of both happiness and sorrow. But it was impossible for me to miss the change that prayer had made in me. I was full of a profound sense of gratitude for the abundance of life that God had given me, an abundance that was above the events of the day, both good and bad. With the hilltops rising to the right of me, and the forest and city and sea unspooling below me to my left, I looked through the windshield toward the blue sky ahead and prayed again that first prayer of mine: *Thank you, God.*

Then I went on. *I don't know how to respond to this abundance,* I told him. *You've given me so much. You've given me everything I wanted since I was a child. Presence of mind and love and a voice and meaning and beauty. You've just handed them to me, gifts, like on Christmas. I don't know how to repay you. I don't know how to begin. You're God and I'm nothing. I can't think of a single thing I can offer you that would matter to you. If there's something I'm missing, tell me. Please. Tell me what you want me to do.*

The answer came back to me on the instant, so clear in my heart it might have been spoken aloud: *Now you should be baptized.*

And I blurted at the windshield: "Baptized? You've got to be kidding me!"

Nothing could have been further from my mind. I thought I had moved beyond all that. Religions, doctrines, scriptures—I figured I had left them all behind. I had formed a personal relationship with the creator of heaven and earth. The last thing I wanted was some church or some preacher yammering at me about what that relationship was supposed to mean, or what rules I should follow or what rites I should perform or really about anything. I still read the Bible from time to time as the mighty and foundational work of literature it was, but I'd never turned to it as a source of anything more than literary wisdom—as I would turn to a Dostoevsky novel or a Shakespeare play—and I had no plans to start now. And really, to go back into all that Jesus business that had driven me so crazy in my youth . . . and to start such an uproar in my family . . . and to make my public opinions even more unacceptable and controversial than they'd already become . . . it was trouble I didn't want and didn't need. And for what? I wasn't a Christian. Was I? I didn't even believe any of the things that Christians are supposed to believe.

What could it mean then: *baptized*? Why should God want that of me now?

At first I tried to dismiss the idea. Perhaps it wasn't a celestial communication, just a fleeting thought of my own. The mind deceives itself, after all. It does nothing better. An angel clothed in radiant light could descend on wings of ivory and whisper the truth of ages in my ear, and I could still get it wrong. That's how corrupt the heart can be.

But one of the most important things I had learned—one of the central principles of my reclamation—was this: the very fact that the mind can be deceived implies that it can be *not* deceived, that it can know things rightly—deep things— beauty, truth—just as they are. The call to baptism had come to me so clearly that I couldn't just ignore it. In all humility, in all gratitude, I had to ask myself: Was this the word of God?

So for the first time since I had started praying, I began to try to put my beliefs about this God I had come to know into words and into order. I tried to define my theology. The result should not have startled me, but it did.

G. K. Chesterton said that in stumbling onto his Christian faith he was like an English yachtsman who had gone off course: he thought that he had discovered a new island when, in fact, he had landed back in England. I saw now that I was like an archaeologist who, after a lifetime of digging, had unearthed the lost foundations of a civilization that turned out, in fact, to be his own. I had spent fifty years of reading and contemplation and seeking and prayer and I had managed to do nothing more than reinvent the Christian wheel.

What were my five epiphanies if not tenets of Christian faith? The truth of suffering was the knowledge of the cross. The wisdom of joy was the soul's realization through relationship with God. The reality of love was the personality of the Creator as only Jesus had ever revealed it. The possibility of clear perception was the sign that we were made in God's image, that we had the ability to know his good as our good, even if only through a glass darkly.

Then there was the laughter at the heart of mourning, my bizarre but ever-present sense that, despite our grief and fear and suffering, some essential comedy lived at the center of tragic existence. What could that be if not the realization that this life is not what we were meant for, that death is not what we were meant for, that who we are is not who we're supposed to be? Even the lowest form of humor—maybe especially the lowest, the most basic form—suggests that we were intended to be something higher than ourselves. A man who slips on a banana peel and falls into a puddle of mud is funny not because of his pain but because of the contrast with his sense of dignity. He feels he is something high, but he has become something low and ridiculous. So it is with us when we sin. So it is with us even when we die. We are meant for something better, and we know it, and even as we suffer and mourn, we also laugh.

In response to the call to baptism, I examined my theology and I saw that—in theory at least, philosophically at least—I was, in fact, a Christian, yes. I believed in the Father, the loving Creator: I had seen his power with my own eyes. I believed in the Holy Spirit, the communication between God and man: I had experienced it for myself through prayer and it had brought my life to fullness. And because I believed that man was made in God's image, I also believed it was possible that, at the right moment in history, a man could be born who was God incarnate. I believed in Christ . . . in theory; philosophically. The possibility of the incarnation followed logically from everything else.

I went home and began to reread the Bible. In the light of these realizations, I understood it in a new way. This great story each life was telling, this great story all history was telling, this story of the spirit all flesh was telling: here it was, beginning, middle, and end. The Bible was the story God wanted to tell us about himself—about himself and us. I'm not a literalist. I believe this book of all books contains different genres: myth, legend, poetry, and history too. It would have to. No single genre could convey all the wisdom it has to convey. But all the genres of the Bible are part of its overall story and, within that context, all are true and uniquely true.

There was, however, one part of the story that had to be absolutely factual in order to verify the truth of the rest: the Gospels. In order for me to accept the call to baptism, it was not enough for me to believe in the *possibility* of Christ—Christ in theory. It was not enough for me to feel—as I did feel—that the Jesus story said fully and precisely and uniquely what I believed to be the truth about God and our relationship with God. For me to accept baptism, the Jesus story had to be true on every level, not just as myth but as myth and history combined. That was the whole point. Christ's life proved and fulfilled the Bible's story of God. For me to accept baptism, I had to believe in Christ's reality—in the reality not just of his life but also of his miracles and death and resurrection.

But how could I? Such things don't happen. Look around you. There are no miracles. There can be no resurrection. The clockwork world is all in all.

But *such things don't happen*, I knew now, was the ultimate irrational prejudice of the human mind: the belief that the symbols of reality are more real than the reality they symbolize. That's us all over. We believe that money is more valuable than the work it represents, that sex is more essential than the love it expresses, that an actor is more admirable than the hero he portrays, that flesh is more alive than spirit. That's the whole nature of our deluded lives, the cause of so much of our misery. One by one, we let idolatry ruin each good thing. Without faith, we can't help ourselves. Without faith, we can no more see through our materialist prejudice than we can see through the big blue bowl of the sky and into the eternity beyond. The choice between idolatry and faith—which is ultimately the choice between slavery in the flesh and freedom in the spirit—is the only real choice we have to make.

I was reading the gospel of Mark when the sky, as you might say, opened, and my own resistance at last gave way. Mark has been called the existential gospel: the unadorned story of Jesus' failure and execution. In the oldest versions we have, the book ends abruptly. Jesus is crucified and buried.

Three of his women followers come to anoint his corpse after the Sabbath. They find his tomb empty. A man dressed in white tells them Christ is risen. The women run away in terror. That's it. That's the end.

Scholars believe that the concluding verses have been lost. That's the way it reads to me too: a jagged finale, edited by time. When I went through it again, it seemed, in this, to have been fashioned by providence to speak to me directly. All my life, God had set the full truth of himself aside in order to reach me in my unbelief—just like the Christian ballplayer who had stopped preaching Jesus long enough to communicate the idea I needed to hear. God had given me the pieces of the puzzle one by one until I could assemble them myself into the picture of that face that had watched over me on my first Christmas Eve. Now he had even torn the last page off his gospel for me and shown me only an empty tomb—something I could accept, something I did accept, something I believed in by this time with all my heart because I knew it made sense of everything else.

I saw the empty tomb and I had faith.

It was now that I began the five months of self-examination that provided the contents of this book. Driving the winding roads through the mountains, taking longer and longer detours to give myself time to pray longer and longer prayers on my way to work, I cross-examined myself endlessly: Was my Christian faith nothing more than some Freudian longing for divine parental love? Was it some sort of angry strike against my father? Was it a Jew's desire for assimilation into the greater culture? Was it the resurgence of an old neurosis? On and on.

Yet, in the end, I found my faith remained. I was, after all, still the boy who insisted that even the stories of his daydreams make sense. The story of Christ's life, death, and resurrection not only made sense in itself, it made sense of everything I had experienced and everything I had come to know. It made sense of the world.

The day I made my mind up, I drove down out of the mountains, wild-eyed—more like a hermit returning from a vision-trek in the wilderness than some suburban guy who had taken the long way round to work. I could hardly believe what had happened to me. I could hardly believe what I was going to do. I sat down at my desk and wrote a rather frantic and inarticulate e-mail to my old friend Father Doug Ousley in New York. I told him I wanted to be baptized. I was afraid that, knowing me as well as he did, he would think I had lost my mind again. He was surprised, in fact. He had thought I was so stubborn I would resist until I was at the point of death.

I broke the news to my wife the next morning as we had our coffee together in bed. Normally, I entertained and amused the poor woman with every thought that went through my head in something like real time. But for some reason, this experience had been different. I had faced the struggle of conversion alone. I did not know how she would react to it.

For most of her life, Ellen had been an atheist, a down-to-earth realist with only a small, and mostly ironic, strain of Irish mysticism in her. When I had first started praying, she hadn't followed me into faith. I used to tease her that since she always adopted my point of view in the long run, she ought to do it right away and save time. Oddly enough, only one of us found this joke amusing.

But about a year before, Ellen herself had been through a dramatic transformation. After a long illness, her mother had died in her arms. Ellen had come home from the experience greatly changed. For days, it was as if there was a nimbus of light around her. Every sentence she spoke was a gem of condensed wisdom. It was like living with some kind of sibyl. She told me she had seen her mother's spirit leave the world. It left a mark on her. She had believed in God ever since.

So she accepted my decision easily. My children did as well.

But I still had to tell my parents and brothers. My mother, I knew, would shrug it off. It was religion. It had no meaning to her, one way or the other. My brothers were sure to greet the news with their usual humor and grace. My father, though . . . it would break his heart. He would feel it as a failure, an insult and a betrayal of his race. It would devastate and infuriate him.

Dad was in his late seventies, still vigorous. Our relations were friendly but distant. When we were together, we made small talk about movies and the latest technology. I never spoke to him about anything that mattered, my family or my feelings or my work.

But there was no way to hide this from him. I was a writer. I lived a public life. There was barely a thought that went through my mind that didn't end up in print somewhere or get mentioned in some interview or other. My being baptized—a secular, intellectual Jew accepting Christ: it was a good story. There was no chance I wasn't going to tell it. As painful as the news might be to my father, it seemed unfair—it seemed unkind—to let him read about it in the newspaper or hear about it from someone he knew.

Around Christmastime, my parents came out west to spend a few winter weeks in Los Angeles. I wrestled with the idea of telling them about my conversion when they came up to visit the grandchildren. How was I going to do it? What was I going to say?

As it turned out, I never got a chance to find the answers to those questions. During their first visit to my house, my father announced that they would have to return to New York at once. He had suddenly developed double vision and he wanted to go to his regular doctor at home for a checkup.

At first, I laughed this off. My father had a neurotic habit of ending trips abruptly this way. He was forever rushing home to deal with some emergency or other that turned out to be either overblown or downright imaginary. This happened so frequently—almost every time he traveled—that I just assumed this to be a typical case, typical to the point of comedy.

I was wrong. My parents returned to New York. My father went to the doctor to have his vision checked. He was diagnosed with a brain tumor.

We were told the condition was treatable. The tumor was a symptom of multiple myeloma, a usually slow-moving blood cancer. The doctors figured that, at nearly eighty, my father might well survive it long enough to die of something else.

Even so, there was, to my mind, no possibility of telling him about my baptism now. If he was dying, it could serve no purpose to break his heart and add fresh sorrow to his final days. If he lived and got better, there would be time to work the matter out between us.

Still, for myself, I needed to move forward. Now that I knew I was a Christian, I had begun going to church. Every Sunday I would walk down to All Saints-by-the-Sea, a lovely little place by the ocean, a few blocks away. I would sit by myself in a rear pew, pray the prayers and sing the songs and listen to the sermon, and then slip out—after the collection but before communion. It wasn't like going to church in the old days of madness, a blind groping after spiritual comfort of some kind. And I was no longer offended by the benign commonplaces of church life or the tuna casseroles. I remained what I was: a daydreaming artist with a woefully irrepressible sense of humor. But I had lost the arrogance of my eccentricities. I saw my own sin and suffering on the face of everyone who prayed, and I understood that tuna casseroles can also be part of the language of love.

In faith, I found the church services tranquil, affecting, and often transporting. But I wanted more. I wanted to be part of the body of Christ. I wanted to take communion. I wanted to be what I was, to live as what I was.

My parents had left Great Neck by now. When their children had grown, they had moved to an apartment in the city as my mother had always wanted. And since Doug Ousley lived in Manhattan, too, my life developed a strange duality.

Every few weeks, I would travel back east. I would go to see my father—to join him at the doctor's office when he went to have the tumor burned out, to visit him as he recovered, to sit and chat with him while he struggled with his failing health. Then I would leave my parents' apartment and walk downtown to the Church of the Incarnation. I would meet Doug at the rectory door and we would head out to some bar we liked and discuss my conversion over a drink.

I didn't need much preparation for baptism. That is to say, I had studied Christianity so much at this point, I could bypass the usual formal classes. I was ready within weeks. But the travel was hard to arrange—and by the time I could get back to the city, there was another delay: Lent. There's no definitive rule against baptism during these weeks of fasting, but most churches wait until after Easter to perform such a joyful rite, especially with adults.

So I waited—and during that Lenten time, my father's health collapsed. The multiple myeloma did not behave as the doctors expected. It wasn't slow at all. It swept through the old man like locusts and devoured him from within. About a week before Easter, I decided I should visit him again. Before I arrived, my older brother warned me with the very words my father had spoken about his own father so long ago: "Prepare yourself. He doesn't look good."

The moment I walked into his apartment and saw him, I knew my father was dying. I had seen people die before and the shadow of the end was on him unmistakably. My mother and my brothers had been with him continually through his decline. I don't think they had registered the full extent of it. I was returning to visit after an absence of several weeks, so it hit me all at once.

I visited with him for a while and then walked out, shaken. As I was heading away down the busy city avenue, my cell phone rang. It was my father's doctor calling . . .

After I found faith, coincidence looked different to me. I'm not saying I detected the hand of God in every odd occurrence or that I knew the meaning of even those events that seemed especially marked by God's presence. But what had appeared accidental to me in the past, now often seemed to bear the imprint of supernatural intent. Once you see it you can't unsee it: the supernatural is not supernatural; the ordinary world is suffused with the miraculous.

Here was an instance. Not long before my father's illness, his old doctor had retired and a new doctor had taken over the practice. It turned out, against every chance, that this doctor was an old friend of mine, a man I liked and respected very much. Our lives had first been bound together by a death—the death of his girlfriend, who was a close friend of my wife's. We were now bound together again by my father.

The doctor did not know I was in town. I hadn't told him I was coming. Yet there he was, calling just as I left my father's place.

"Have you seen your dad recently? How's he doing?" he asked.

"Well, you're the one who went to med school," I said. "But to me, he looks like he's dying."

When I hung up with him, I called my older brother and told him the same thing. My brother said he would go to my father's apartment and see how things stood.

A few hours later, I went to see Doug. We went to a tavern near Bryant Park to make final plans for my baptism. Just as the priest and I were settling into our seats by the window, my cell phone rang. It was my brother. He had taken my father to the hospital.

My mother and brothers and I gathered there at my father's bedside. We didn't think this was the end, not at first. The doctors still held out hope. I had been planning to fly home the next day, so I canceled my flight and rescheduled it for a day later—and then again, for a day later—and then for another day after that.

With the effortless symbolism of reality, we now entered both Holy Week and the week of Passover. Holy Week, of course, marks the end of Lent, and the prelude to Easter Sunday. The week commemorates Jesus' final days, his triumphal entry into Jerusalem, his last supper with his disciples, his arrest and trial and crucifixion. These events had originally taken place at Passover, the Jews' celebration of their great liberation from Egyptian slavery. Jesus came to Jerusalem to mark that celebration. His last supper was a Passover meal. Because both Easter and Passover are movable feasts, the holidays have broken apart from each other but continue to circle around the same few weeks of the calendar—separated but forever linked, like the religions they represent. This year, they came together as my father was dying.

Day by day, my father declined. Palm Sunday into Holy Monday, then Tuesday and Wednesday. At first he could speak to us a little, drawing down his oxygen mask with a trembling hand to whisper hoarsely. After a while, he was too weak to do even that. At one point, he seized my older brother's hand in his and drew it down to the mask to kiss it goodbye.

He died in the early hours of Maundy Thursday, the day of Christ's last Passover.

For twenty-five years, my father had been one of the most popular radio entertainers in the city, first with his partner Dee Finch and then for many years alone. His off-beat and antic sense of humor and his extraordinary gift for creating funny voices and accents made his show avant-garde and unique. It's still considered something of a classic among aficionados of the medium.

The show went off the air in 1977. I was twenty-three then. I was living in New York so I went over to the station to watch the final hour. Engineers and newsmen and other DJs had gathered in the studio for a farewell party. Early in the morning though it was, we were all drinking champagne out of paper cups.

As the show was drawing to a close, the crowd grew boisterous and noisy. The studio—usually hushed so as not to interfere with the performer on mike—was now loud with talk and laughter. Like most radio guys of that time, my father had a sign-on and sign-off line that he was known by: "Morning there, you." As the clock hand reached the top of the hour, I moved close to him so I could hear him say it for the last time.

He did say it—but just before the news came on, he leaned in close to the microphone, and in a voice so low it was almost drowned out by the chatter around us, he whispered: "I love you, New York."

He did love that city. Not its wealth or its high fashion or its halls of power. He loved the chaos of it. The obstreperous little-guy take-a-hike attitude of the individual tough guys and tough girls in the neighborhoods and warehouses and shops and subways and cabs. The Nazis were always on the march, remember, always coming for us, just beneath the horizon line, just around the bend, stomping in unison, black boots polished and brown shirts pressed, all in perfect order, bringing nothing but death. It was only city-street chaos and the little man's spit-in-your-eye that held those monsters at bay. Jews and Italians and Irish one generation; blacks and Asians and Arabs the next. Dad didn't care. Just so long as they kept the chaos going, passed it down to each other like the precious inheritance it was. The cacophony of the city's angry, unruly, and hilarious voices spoke to him, and one by one he spoke those voices back: his chaos to their chaos, their characters peopling the carnival of his mind.

I walked Manhattan's streets in the early morning of the day he died. From the East River, along Forty-second to Broadway and down to Herald Square. I felt his spirit hovering over the rising stone, loath to go.

I stayed in town another day to help my brothers with the death arrangements. I flew back to California on Saturday. The next day was Easter. My wife and I walked down to All

Saints-by-the-Sea. We sat in a pew near the back. I was mystic with exhaustion. The light through the stained-glass windows seemed to fall on the altar lilies with a strangely golden glow and the golden glow seemed strangely to envelop me.

I was glad to be here, where I belonged, glad to celebrate even in mourning this joy of joys: the resurrection and the life. My heart was weary but no longer sad and all around me there were hallelujahs.

CHAPTER 14

A New Story

A month or so after my father died, I returned to New York for his memorial and for my baptism.

The memorial was a small gathering of family and friends in the outdoor courtyard of a Manhattan restaurant near my parents' apartment. I hadn't seen most of these people in years, in decades some of them. They were people I liked and who had loved my father and it was good to have them there. But seeing them after all this time was also a bittersweet reminder of how distant I had become from my parents and their lives and from the life of my childhood.

At one point during the memorial, as I found myself standing alone for a moment, an old man came toward me through the crowd. He was very bent and fragile, leaning on a cane, making his way unsteadily across the court. I didn't know him. When we were face-to-face, he spoke to me. He said he had worked with my father at the radio station in the old days, near the beginning of my father's New York career.

The moment he started talking, I recognized his voice. He had a thick New York Yiddish accent that sounded exactly like my father's much beloved character Mr. Nat. Mr. Nat—that was the exuberant Coordinator of Interrelations who used to make my mother shudder with assimilationist horror every time he came on the air: "I wish you wouldn't do that character!" I fancied my father must have modeled Nat's voice on the voice of this man standing in front of me. The accent, the pitch, the tone—they were Mr. Nat to perfection.

As the man spoke, a whimsical thought occurred to me. I remembered how my father used to call home from the city sometimes with a disguised voice as a kind of prank on us kids. It occurred to me that maybe he was calling home again now, this time from that unseen city from which no traveler returns.

And just as that thought occurred to me, this old man, whom I didn't know, and who didn't know me, said in his Mr. Nat voice, "Your father wanted you to be a Jew. He was always afraid you didn't want to be a Jew. He was always afraid you didn't like being a Jew. He wanted you to be a Jew."

Then he turned and wobbled away and moved out of sight among all the others.

My baptism was scheduled for the next evening.

I smiled sadly to myself and nodded. I knew what the old man said was true. Only my father's death had saved me from breaking his heart by my conversion. But I knew also it couldn't be any other way. I could not both journey to myself and stay here with him.

The next evening, I made my way to the Church of the Incarnation. The light of the spring day was fading when I arrived. The brownstone steeple was blending with the darkening sky. Inside, the scarlets and azures and bright yellows of the stained-glass windows along the wall were losing their vividness as the sunlight fell away from them. The vast, high spaces of the church seemed filled with an uncanny blue aura, a dusk that hung between the white columns and underneath the carving on the elaborate altarpiece: "And the Word was made flesh."

As I mentioned before, the rector, my friend Doug Ousley, had indulged my penchant for privacy by opening the church after hours. When I first came in, the place seemed empty. Then I saw Doug and his family, down in the front pews, off to the left by the John the Baptist font. Doug was in his priestly regalia. Mary had now been brought down into a wheelchair by her disease. She managed to smile and murmur a few words of affection to me as I leaned over to kiss her. Her blue eyes still flashed, still showed traces of the loving and vivacious woman she had been when I first met her. She had only a few years left to live now. Tonight, she would serve as my godmother.

And, of course, the Ousleys' grown sons John and Andrew were there, clowning around as always, making their usual sardonic jokes. John, only a year or two older than my daughter, was going to serve as my godfather. They thought this was hilarious.

"We will light a candle to symbolize the light of Christ in your spirit," Doug explained to me. "And at the end of the service, the candle will be extinguished—"

"And your spirit will be snuffed out," Andrew muttered.

I nearly fell out of the pew laughing. We were all in very good spirits.

These friends were there with me—but not my family, not my own wife and my own children. I had sent them home, back to California, after my father's memorial. It was a decision I would come to regret almost immediately after the ritual was over. It was then I would realize that, all too typically of myself, I had made exactly the same mistake I had made nearly twenty-five years before at my wedding. As I had once believed Ellen and I were already essentially married and that our wedding was simply a formality, so now I believed my heart was already baptized and this was just a rite to symbolize the event. It was as if—as I would remark ruefully before the evening was over—as if I had learned absolutely nothing in all the intervening years.

Now that I have experienced this last decade of life in Christ—the peace and realism of Christ, the hope and truth—I think even this error was part of the story God was telling me. He was using my own foolishness as a parable, just the sort of satiric parable he knew I would appreciate and understand.

Because now I knelt at the baptismal font, beneath the upraised hand of the bronze boy John. Now Doug put the water on my head, the oil on my brow, and spoke the words: "I baptize you in the name of the Father and of the Son and of the Holy Spirit." Now I climbed to my feet again and looked around me at the faces of my friends in the church's mysterious gloaming.

And now I saw. I had been wrong—yet once more. I had been wrong about baptism as I was wrong about my wedding. It mattered. It mattered in ways I could not understand until the very moment I had done it. Of course. I should have known. Who more than me? Ritual and transition, symbol and reality, story and life—they are intimately intertwined forever. They are the language of the imagination, the language in which God speaks to man.

Well, mine is a stiff-necked people, slow to learn. Yet just as with my wedding, here I was somehow. Through my own foolishness and the foolishness of my times, through the fog of my egotism and stubbornness and insanity, God had sung to me without ceasing in the stories I loved and in my love and in my story. I, even half-blind with myself, had stumbled after that music to its source.

And somehow, once again, by the hilarious mercy of God, I had made my way to the great good thing.

ACKNOWLEDGMENTS

Before I began this memoir, I would have said, if asked, that my work was my life. Having finished, it now seems to me that, in fact, my life was my work: a work assigned to the author by his Author, the work of journeying to a true faith. As I wrote the scenes of my biography, I was startled—stunned sometimes—to discover how often God had been openly present in those scenes and yet invisible to the man he was beckoning, guiding, and guarding. It was a story I didn't know I was telling until I told it. I was grateful to God before. I'm doubly grateful now.

There was another aspect of the story I did understand from the beginning. If this memoir sometimes reads like a love letter to my wife, Ellen, it's because it is. For nearly forty years, she has been my muse, my song, my soul, my only-ever love. I could not have survived the troubles detailed here, nor have experienced the joys, without her.

And I could not have written this book. The first draft was a sloppy monster, twice as long as this. I'd never attempted a long-form non-fiction work before, and I guess I threw in everything I could think of. My wife, always my first reader and editor, went through it and told me, "Half of this is the best book you've ever written." She then took nearly two weeks out of her busy life to show me, page by page, how to cut it down to its present size. In doing this, she made the book half as long and twice as good. And yes, I noticed she didn't cut out any of the encomia to herself, but what would have been the point? I only would have put them back again.

My thanks to her, as always.

My thanks also to Webster Younce, my editor at HarperCollins, who patiently talked the book through with me before I began writing, helped me as I worked along the way, and then edited the final version. I should also thank HarperCollins Christian Fiction publisher Daisy Hutton, who listened to my story over dinner one evening and said, "You should tell that story to Webster." I'm glad I did.

Thank you, too, to Don Fehr, my non-fiction agent at Trident Media, for taking on a stranger from the fiction department and representing him so well.

Thank you to my son, Spencer, for reading a draft, discussing some of the ideas with me, and guiding me on matters of Greek translation and culture.

And finally to my friend Father Douglas Ousley, rector of the Church of the Incarnation in Manhattan: thank you for some timely enlightenment on Christian doctrine. And for the baptism.

Notes

Chapter 2: Addicted to Dreams

1. Bizarrely enough, the house eventually attracted a real-life horror. About ten years after I left town, a family of child molesters moved in, the subject of a famous documentary film entitled *Capturing the Friedmans*.

Chapter 4: A Christmas Carol

1. Comedian Jon Lovitz would later create a similar character with the same name on the TV show *Saturday Night Live*, but my dad beat him to it by about a quarter of a century.

Chapter 5: Tough Guys

1. Some articles say *Vertigo* was never aired. I think they're wrong. But my father sometimes brought home movies and showed them on a projector in our basement. It's possible I saw it that way. In any case, I saw the film when I was young.
2. Raymond Chandler, *The Big Sleep* (New York: Alfred A. Knopf, 1939).
3. Raymond Chandler, *The Simple Art of Murder* (New York: Houghton Mifflin, 1950).

4. *Raymond Chandler Speaking*, ed. by Dorothy Gardiner and Kathrine Sorley Walker (Berkeley: University of California Press, 1962).

Chapter 7: Experience

1. In developing this technique, I was ahead of my time. I suspect many university English professors and newspaper literary critics are using it today.

Chapter 10: Going Crazy

1. M. H. Abrams, *Natural Supernaturalism: Tradition and Revolution in Romantic Literature* (New York: Norton, 1971).

Chapter 11: Five Epiphanies

1. John Keats, "Ode on a Grecian Urn," poets.org. This poem is in the public domain.
2. Marquis de Sade, *Philosophy in the Bedroom* (New York: Grove Press, 1971).

About the Author

Andrew Klavan is the author of internationally best-selling crime novels such as *True Crime*, filmed by Clint Eastwood, *Don't Say a Word*, filmed starring Michael Douglas, and *Empire of Lies*. He has been nominated for the Mystery Writers of America's Edgar Award five times and has won twice. He has also won the Thumping Good Read Award from WH Smith and been nominated twice for the Bouchercon's Anthonys. His Young Adult novels include the bestselling Homelanders series. His books have been translated around the world. As a screenwriter, Andrew wrote the screenplays for *Shock to the System*, starring Michael Caine; *One Missed Call*, starring Ed Burns; and the award-winning movie-in-an-app *Haunting Melissa*. He is a contributing editor to *City Journal*, and his essays have appeared in the *Wall Street Journal*, the *New York Times*, the *LA Times*, and elsewhere. He also writes and appears in several popular series of satirical online videos, including *Klavan on the Culture* and *The Revolting Truth*. He lives in Los Angeles with his wife, Ellen.